PEEK-A-BOO FOOTWORK

Sam Ness

«PEEK-A-BOO: FOOTWORK»

Footwork is the most important skill of a boxer. The author explains the technique of footwork used by peekaboo boxers, the most famous style of boxing in the XXth century. Based on biomechanics, the author gives a detailed description of various footwork tricks. Peekaboo footwork allows a boxer to create angles in boxing, switch stances, shift to the flanks and catch opponents with unexpected southpaw punches. That's what Mike Tyson was known for.

The book contains a lot of photos, which frame-by-frame illustrate the technique of movement. Using peekaboo footwork, a boxer will inject real dynamism into his offensive boxing style.

The book is intended for trainers, professional boxers, and amateurs, as well as boxing fans.

Copyright © 2023 **Sam Ness**
Author: **S. Ness**
ISBN: 9798375064741
Imprint: Independently published

CONTENTS

PEEKABOO FOOTWORK AND BIOMECHANICS

Footwork

It's a very simple fact that good footwork is the beginning, the middle, and the end of boxing. All top boxers possess great footwork and balance. Footwork is the concept used to describe how a boxer moves around a boxing ring, changes position, and approaches an opponent. Skillful footwork allows a boxer to always be in an advantageous position to attack and defend. Developing superb boxing footwork is an absolute requirement for reaching the peak of boxing mastery.

All kinds of movements characteristic of boxing are used in peekaboo. A special role in peekaboo plays jumping and leaping movements. Besides, it should be noted that footwork is improved with the development of boxing. It also concerns the peekaboo style. For example, Floyd Patterson's peekaboo footwork differs from Michael Tyson's peekaboo footwork in many ways.

The footwork technique was constantly improved. The addition of jumping movements made it possible to shorten the distance very quickly by combining it with pendulum body movements. This was exactly what Patterson lacked in his fights with Muhammad Ali. Ali easily stopped Patterson's attacks at middle and long range.

The technique of moving after Floyd Patterson has been significantly improved. At long range, the main goal was to get close to an opponent quickly and shorten the distance. At medium and close range, the main aim was to move away from the line of attack, to move relative to an opponent, and to change the angles of attack. To achieve these goals, various types of jumps and leaps were used.

In its most complete form, the peekaboo footwork is reflected in the technique of Michael Tyson. A characteristic feature of Mike Tyson's peekaboo movements was the active cutting of angles when attacking and defending. Mike attacked from one side, immediately moving after the attack. As a result of the new training methodology, Michael Tyson became a very mobile boxer, with very good foot coordination. Modern footwork of peekaboo is very dynamic and requires good coordination, high endurance, and agility.

Gravity and footwork

Gravity plays an important role in the peekaboo footwork. This force attracts to the Earth. Gravity also acts on the body of a boxer. It is an excellent aid for footwork. Boxers can use the force of gravity in various footwork techniques. This takes the strain off the leg muscles and makes jumping easier and faster. Gravity is one source of dynamics.

The boxer's ability to control the center of the body and sense of balance is very important for footwork. A boxer must use gravity in his movements to enhance and accelerate his jumps. Using gravity in the footwork facilitates the muscular work of the legs. It is one thing for a boxer to perform footwork techniques by the muscular power of the legs and it is quite another thing to perform footwork techniques using gravity.

Peak controlled points of instability

The basis for using gravitational force in the footwork is the displacement of the body center beyond the area of support. Such points in the dynamics of a fight can be called the peak controlled points of instability. The peak point is because it is the extreme point of balance, after which a boxer loses his balance. The controlled point is because a boxer consciously creates such instability and controls the balance in it.

At the peak controlled points of instability, a boxer is on the verge of falling and balance. At such points of controlled instability, the action of gravity can easily break a boxer's equilibrium. Breaking this equilibrium will cause a boxer to «fall», which can be used for rapid jumps and moves.

To create unstable equilibrium and invoke gravity, a boxer must artificially bring the center of his body to the boundary of the support area or slightly beyond it. As if a boxer begins to fall.

During a fight, peak equilibrium points are easily created as a result of the defensive peekaboo technique. Any slipping, bobbing or ducking position creates a charged structure. Boxer groups all muscles of the body for movement. In doing so, any slip to the left or right, a crouch, can be combined with the creation of a disequilibrium point where there is a threat of loss of balance (in other words the action of gravity).

Thus, if a boxer in the slipping position creates a controlled point of instability and induces gravitational force, then good conditions are formed for jumping and leaping. In this case, a boxer will move both by muscle strength and by the force of the fall.

Charged structure and footwork

In reality, footwork techniques are both a combination of free-fall force and the strength of own muscles used to accelerate the body weight. Before any footwork trick, it is necessary to create a charged body structure that groups the muscles for explosive movements. A charged body structure is created by slipping, ducking or bobbing. In this case, all muscles in the body are ready to move explosively and powerfully. A spring in the body is charged and the pushing force from the ground necessary for the leap is generated. Examples of charged structures are shown in the photos below.

The work of the body in the peekaboo creates an excellent biomechanical basis for boxing footwork. According to the laws of biodynamics, jumps are very convenient to do in combination with slips and squats. Slips transfer the body weight from leg to leg and thus turn it into a pushing leg, charging the body for a jump and thus helping a boxer to make the jump without any extra effort. Thus, besides their protective functions, defensive maneuvers are seen as preliminary body movements for various footwork techniques. Defensive maneuvers facilitate footwork maneuvers.

Angle theory and footwork

The theory of angles in boxing is a set of techniques that allow a boxer to change the angle of attack to deliver a strong and unexpected blow to an opponent. It is impossible to change the angle of attack without footwork. It is thanks to the footwork techniques that a boxer can quickly change his position concerning his opponent and thereby change the angle of attack.

Another advantage of angle attacks is that an opponent does not see coming blows and so these are the knockout punches. Thanks to the techniques of footwork, a boxer moves relative to an opponent on the flanks, goes out of an opponent's field of vision, and attacks at new angles. As a result, it is difficult for an opponent to defend against such blows.

It is possible to change the angles of attack only by footwork. In this book, we will discuss various patterns of changing angles of attack using different footwork tricks. The footwork allows boxers to take an angle advantage. It means taking such a position where an opponent can't hit easily, but a boxer has many options to land punches. The most obvious examples of an angle advantage are when a boxer is behind or from the left or right side of his opponent. From there, a boxer can land hooks to the head or the body while his opponent can't. That's because a boxer is off the center line and in a safe position. It's hard to get on flanks but it's possible when a boxer has good footwork.

It is very important to choose the right moment to change angles. Usually, the angles are cut when an opponent's attention is distracted or an opponent covers up and cannot see the boxer. Such situations can be created by various deceptive actions and additional preliminary blows before moving to the flanks. There are various patterns of changing angles with preliminary deceptive actions. These include false slips, preliminary deceptive blows, significant speed, changes of rhythm and extra steps. These all cause an opponent to become confused and use the momentum to cut the angles. Most of these patterns are reviewed in the book.

Jumping and leaping movements

The main methods by which a boxer can quickly change the angle of attack are jumps and leaps. Jumps and leaps are explosive footwork. Before describing the main types of jumps and leaps, it is necessary to give an initial classification. This classification is very simple and is based on which leg is the pushing one. The biomechanics of the movement of the human body is based on the fact that most often one leg is the pushing leg and the other leg is used to land after a push. Therefore, being in the basic stance, a boxer can use either his left or right leg to push. Hence, there are two options for jumps, depending on which leg a boxer pushes.

The first group of jumps is where a boxer pushes with his lead foot in stance. The second group of jumps is in which a boxer pushes off with his rear foot in stance.

Also, the biomechanics of the human body allows jumping by pushing with two feet. Concerning boxing, this is the case when a boxer is in the lower stance with his legs bent, then two feet are pushing at the same time. This is the third group of jumps.

The second classification feature for jumps is the direction of the moves. Based on the tactical placement of the two boxers, a boxer can make a jump in several directions.

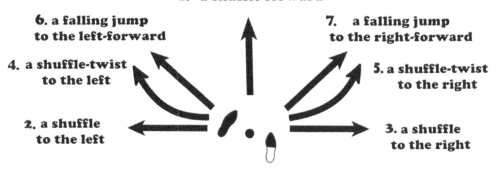

1. a shuffle forward

6. a falling jump to the left-forward

7. a falling jump to the right-forward

4. a shuffle-twist to the left

5. a shuffle-twist to the right

2. a shuffle to the left

3. a shuffle to the right

Of course, we can also consider jumps back. But based on that peekaboo is an attacking style whose goal is to get closer to an opponent, we will consider only those directions that allow a boxer to get closer to an opponent, cut the angles of attack, go on the flanks or switch stance.

An orthodox and a southpaw stance

In terms of the occupied stance in a fight, there are two types of boxers. They are right-handed boxers and left-handed boxers.

Right-handed boxer - a boxer whose right hand is stronger. He prefers to box in the left-side stance, that is, turning the left side of his body to an opponent and putting his left leg forward. «Orthodox» (or a left-side stance) is a boxing stance for a right-handed boxer.

Left-handed boxer – a boxer whose left hand is stronger. He prefers to box in the right-side stance. Left-handed boxer usually turns the right side of his body to an opponent putting his right leg forward. «Southpaw» (or a right-side stance) is a boxing stance for a left-handed boxer.

Most often fighters box in one of the stances depending on their strong hand. But some boxers can switch stances in a fight. The ability to switch stances from an orthodox to a southpaw is a professional and highly qualified boxer's skill. Not all boxers are able to do that. At the same time, the switch of stance is an unexpected maneuver for an opponent and can confuse him. The ability to change stances is an advantage in a fight.

It is well known that the skill of hitting equally hard with both right and left hands was practiced in peekaboo boxing. This is achieved by special exercises, including the work on the «Willie bag». That is why peekaboo boxers often change their stance from an orthodox to a southpaw. The ability to beat strongly with both hands is the basis for switching stances in a fight. If a right-handed boxer can't hit hard with his left hand, it probably makes no sense for him to switch to a southpaw stance.

Changing and switching a stance

Changing the angle of attack is done by changing the stance. In order to change the stance, a boxer needs footwork. A boxer can change his stance through different maneuvers and different methods of footwork. More often than not, the change of stance occurs from the initial orthodox stance. The change of stance can take place both from an orthodox stance to a southpaw stance, and from an orthodox stance to an orthodox stance, but at a different angle to the opponent.

By changing the stance we mean moving the boxer relative to the opponent, taking a new position and changing the angle of attack. After changing the stance, the boxer can keep the orthodox stance or switch to a southpaw stance. The photos below show changes in stance and changes in the angle of attack, both by switching to a southpaw and by keeping the orthodox stance.

By switching the stance, we mean changing from an orthodox stance to a southpaw stance. Switching stance is a particular case for changing the stance. The photos below show examples of changing the angle of attack by switching the stance from an orthodox to a southpaw stance.

Loaded leg after changing a stance

The loaded leg is the leg that carries most of the weight of the boxer at the moment. More often than not, the loaded leg determines the hand that is charged for the punch. After the foot maneuver, the boxer may find himself with a different loaded leg. The moment of landing determines which leg will be loaded and therefore which hand will be striking hand after changing the stance.

Below are examples of changes in stance and angle of attack while maintaining the orthodox stance. In the first case, after one of the footwork tricks, the boxer is in the orthodox stance with the loaded left leg, respectively the body is charged to strike with the left hand.

In the second case, after one of the footwork techniques, the boxer is in an orthodox stance with his body weight on his right foot. Accordingly, the body is charged to strike with the right hand.

The same thing happens when a boxer changes the angle of attack by switching the stance from orthodox to the right-side stance. There are different types of stance switching. In some cases, after switching to a southpaw stance, the lead right leg is charged. Correspondingly, the body is charged to strike with the right hand.

In other cases, after changing stance to the southpaw, the rear left leg is charged. Correspondingly, the body is charged to strike with the left hand.

Understanding the loaded leg is very important for understanding the subsequent hard blow and for building a punching combination after changing the stance. Because the angles are changed by footwork only to deliver a knockout punch quickly and unexpectedly.

THE BASIC ELEMENTS OF FOOTWORK

BOUNCING

A common technique of peekaboo footwork, as well as boxing in general, is bouncing. Bouncing is light springy bounces up and down and simultaneously back and forth or side to side to keep the opponent at a distance and be constantly charged for further action. The essence of this technique is as follows:

1. The feet are approximately shoulder width apart.

2. A boxer puts his weight on his toes and bends his knees slightly.

3. A boxer bounces up and down slightly by bending and unbending his ankle and knee joints.

At the same time, the bouncing is not very high. The feet are off the floor only enough so that a boxer can make short jumps in different directions. A boxer jumps up and down and simultaneously shifts to different sides relative to an opponent depending on the dynamics of the fight. The whole body is maximally relaxed and the legs are as if they were springs which let a boxer make short and not high jumps. The body weight is distributed evenly between the legs.

The best exercise for developing the bouncing technique is jumping rope. The technique allows a boxer to be constantly dynamic and ready for any more complex footwork maneuvers and position changes.

STEPS AND SHIFTS

During the fight, a boxer can't bounce all the time, because it's a rather energy-consuming footwork technique. Therefore, a boxer often switches to different types of steps. Different steps and shifts also allow to prepared footwork tricks. The steps move the body weight from foot to foot and charge the body for the explosive jump or leap.

Ordinary steps

At a long distance, in order to approach an opponent, a boxer uses the usual steps that is used in normal life. A boxer walks forward, backward, left, right, in diagonal directions.

Below is a demonstration of how a boxer gets close to his opponent using ordinary steps. First, the boxer takes a step forward with his right foot, keeping his hands guarded. Then the boxer takes a step forward with his left foot.

Execution by Mike Tyson

Below is an example of when Tyson approaches his opponent using the usual steps forward. He takes a step with his right foot, then a step with his left foot, moving from the far distance to the middle distance.

Step and drag («Louis shuffle»)

When approaching an opponent at a long and medium distances, a boxer uses a «step and drug» technique:

1. A boxer takes a short step forward with the lead foot.
2. A boxer pulls up the rear foot, restoring the stance.

The essence of this movement is a series of very small steps of 4-5 cm with the feet sliding on the floor in a boxing stance. Firstly, without leaving the floor, the left foot slides forward (no more than 4-5 cm) and the right foot follows instantly by the same distance, also without leaving the floor. The knees should be relaxed. A boxer moves with short movements. The left foot stands entirely on the floor. The toe of the right foot also stands firmly on the floor.

When moving by the «step and drug» technique, a boxer's feet should never leave the floor and should always be in a position ready for a sudden attack or defensive maneuver.

It is believed that this type of movement is probably borrowed from fencing. It was used very skillfully by Joe Louis, for which it is called the «Louis shuffle».

The «Louis shuffle» or «step and drug» gives the impression of a boxer walking a tightrope while maintaining balance and balancing the body by slightly slipping.

Execution by Mike Tyson

Tyson takes a small step with his left foot forward and pulls his right foot up. Balancing on the verge of losing his balance, Tyson purposely creates peak points of instability and the threat of losing his balance. At these peaks, the body is in danger of falling. There is a force of gravity acting on the body. The boxer has only to use this force to redirect it into a punch or an explosive jump to change the angle of attack.

Performing the «step and drag» technique, the boxer balances and looks for the peak points of instability where gravity begins to act on his body to the maximum, threatening to fall. Left-right slips charge the boxer's body for explosive jumps and leaps.

Once these conditions coincide, the boxer pushes off the ground, throwing his body mass into free fall under gravity, and shifts relative to his opponent, changing his stance and angle of attack.

Step backward

If it is necessary to break the distance with an opponent, a boxer steps backward according to the scheme «step and drag».

1. A boxer in the stance pushes back with his left (lead) foot and takes a step backward with his right (rear) foot.

2. Then a boxer pulls his left (lead) foot up and restores the stance.

Execution by Jose Torez

The photos below show Jose Torez stepping backward with his right foot and pulling up his left foot.

Footwork and slips

Most of the slips are done with steps. Therefore, combinations of steps and slips are an integral part of the footwork. The basic technique of footwork is to move forward quickly with steps and slips. A boxer can use the slipping technique with steps to get closer to an opponent. The technique is as follows.

1.   A boxer slips to the left by stepping to the left-forward with the left foot.

2.   Immediately boxer slips to the right by stepping to the right-forward with the right foot.

Slips and steps are made until approaching an opponent and reaching the punching range, after which a punching combination is delivered.

Footwork and bob and weave

The next basic tool of peekaboo footwork is the «bob and weave» technique by stepping forward. It can be used to approach an opponent and chase an opponent. To do this, a boxer uses short steps with the left and right foot while bobbing and weaving to the left and right. The technique is as follows.

1. A boxer shifts his body weight to the left leg, rounds the back, and ducks the body slightly forward.

2. Simultaneously, a boxer takes a step to the right-forward with the right foot and then weaves to the right, transferring the body weight to the right leg.

3. Then, a boxer sharply squats on his right leg throwing his left foot slightly forward at the same time.

4. A boxer ducks the body slightly forward and weaves to the left, transferring the body weight to the left leg.

5.   A boxer continues such movements until reaching the punching range with an opponent.

SECTION 3. PIVOT

PIVOT

If necessary to change position relative to an opponent by step, a boxer performs the «pivot» technique. There are two directions to pivot in boxing.

PIVOT CLOCKWISE

1. A boxer shifts his body weight on the balls of his left foot.

2. A boxer turns clockwise on the balls of his left foot (analogy of the circular movement of a compass) into a 45° angle.

3. Simultaneously, a boxer slides his rear right foot to the left behind the lead left foot into a new position.

Execution by Jose Torres

In the photos below, Jose Torres shifts his weight to his lead left foot. He turns sharply clockwise, rotating on the balls of his left foot, and steps with his rear right foot to the left behind his lead right foot. Thus, Torez changes his angle of attack and position relative to his opponent.

The clockwise pivot is biomechanically combined with a slip to the left. Below, a boxer slips to the left and then performs a clockwise pivot.

Also, to create a new angle of attack, a boxer can step preliminary to the left or the left-forward with the left foot, slipping to the left.

Feature. Pivot does not bring the boxer closer to the opponent, but only changes the angle of attack.

PIVOT COUNTERCLOCKWISE

1. A boxer shifts his body weight on the balls of his left foot.

2. A boxer turns counterclockwise on the balls of his left foot (analogy of the circular movement of a compass) into a 45° angle.

3. Simultaneously, a boxer slides his rear right foot to the right behind the lead left foot into a new position.

In some cases, a boxer may preliminary step to the right-forward with his left foot before pivoting counterclockwise. This is a difficult version of the counterclockwise pivot, as for a moment a boxer's feet are crossed, which can threaten stability and balance. Therefore, this is a fairly advanced method of footwork used by skilled boxers.

1. A boxer takes a step to the right-forward with his left foot, ducking to the right.

2. A boxer shifts his body weight on the balls of his left foot.

3. A boxer turns counterclockwise on the balls of his left foot (analogy of the circular movement of a compass) into a 45° angle.

4. Simultaneously, a boxer slides his rear right foot to the right behind the lead left foot into a new position.

Another variation of the counterclockwise pivot is to step previously to the right-forward with the right foot, slipping to the right. After pivoting in this case, the stance is switched from orthodox to a southpaw stance. Switching to a southpaw stance, require further action in that stance. Not every boxer can box in a southpaw stance, so this footwork tool can also be classified as an advanced footwork technique.

1. A boxer takes a step to the right-forward with the right foot, slipping to the right.

2. A boxer shifts his body weight on the balls of his right foot.

3. A boxer turns counterclockwise on the balls of his right foot (analogy of the circular movement of a compass) into a 45° angle.

4. Simultaneously, a boxer slides his rear left foot to the right behind the lead right foot into a new position.

DEMPSEY'S SHIFT

This type of footwork can be called the «Dempsey's shift», as it was often used by Jack Dempsey. A similar movement technique was often used by Tyson. Dempsey performed this movement with both left foot and right foot, respectively let's call them «Dempsey's shift with the left foot» and «Dempsey's shift with the right foot». Let us consider the technique of this type of footwork.

DEMPSEY'S SHIFT WITH THE RIGHT FOOT

Basic technique

At the heart of this footwork technique is the bob and weave defense technique. The essence is as follows:

1.   A boxer ducks, bending the body to the left-forward, transferring the body weight on the left leg.

2.   At the same time, the right foot slides forward, and a boxer switches to the right-side stance.

3.   The body structure charges to the left-hand blow.

This kind of footwork is used to get close to an opponent, to move away from the line of attack, to change the angle of attack, and to accelerate the body weight preliminary due to the bob-and-weave technique.

When at a long distance and the need to get close to an opponent, a boxer may previously take a step with his left foot forward.

1. A boxer takes a step forward with the left foot, cutting the distance with an opponent.

2. A boxer ducks, bending the body to the left-forward, transferring the body weight on the left leg.

3. At the same time, the right foot slides forward, and a boxer switches to the right-side stance.

4. The body structure charges to the left-hand blow.

SECTION 4. DEMPSEY'S SHIFT

Punching technique and Dempsey's shift with the right foot

«Dempsey's shift» is a great way to accelerate the body mass and hit the opponent from a new angle. Blows using this type of footwork are very powerful.

1. The boxer ducks bending the body to the left-forward, transferring the body weight on the left leg.

2. At the same time, the right foot slides forward, and the boxer switches to the right-side stance.

3. The boxer weaves to the right. The body weight is transferred to the right leg.

4. In the final phase of the motion, the boxer delivers one of the possible blows (left hook to the head, left hook to the body, left uppercut).

Execution by Mike Tyson

Tyson takes a step forward with his right foot, ducking to the left-forward. The body weight is shifted to the left leg, and Tyson charges the left side of the body for the punch. The step allows Tyson to get closer to the opponent and to change his stance, and therefore the angles of attack. To protect himself from the possible blows of his opponent when approaching Tyson covers himself with his right forearm like a shield. Tyson takes a southpaw stance. From this position, using the inertia of Dempsey's shift with the right foot forward, Tyson lands an uppercut to the head.

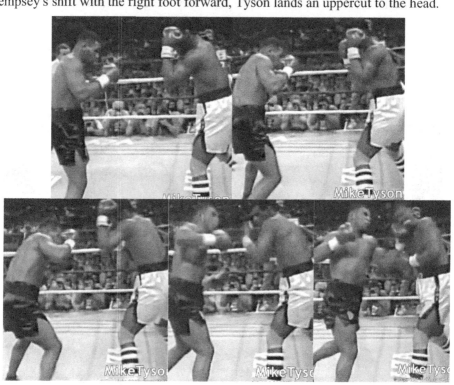

Execution by Mike Tyson

The above footwork technique is confirmed by the sequence of photos presented below. Tyson steps forward with his left foot and then ducks to the left-forward. Then he steps with his right foot forward and weaves to the right, delivering the left hook to the body.

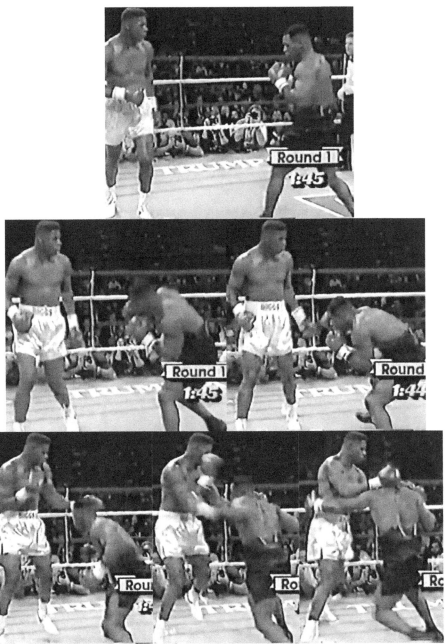

Execution by Mike Tyson

Another example of Dempsey's shift with the right foot is in the photos below. Tyson steps forward with his left foot and then ducks to the left-forward against the opponent's jab. Then he steps with his right foot forward and weaves to the right, delivering the left hook to the opponent's head.

DEMPSEY'S SHIFT WITH THE LEFT FOOT

Basic technique

Similarly, Dempsey's shift is performed on the opposite side as well.

1. A boxer ducks bending the body to the right-forward, transferring the body weight on the right leg.

2. At the same time, the left foot slides forward.

3. The body structure charges to the right-hand blow.

To get close to an opponent, a boxer may previously take a step to the right-forward with his right foot, slipping to the right (the shift to the right).

Punching technique and Dempsey's shift with the left foot

This kind of footwork is used to get close to the opponent, to move away from the line of attack, to accelerate the body weight preliminarily thanks to the bob-and-weave technique, and to blow at the end of the movement.

1. The boxer ducks bending the body to the right-forward, transferring the body weight on the right leg.

2. At the same time, the left foot slides forward.

3. At the same time, the left foot slides forward.

4. The boxer weaves to the right. The body weight is transferred to the left leg.

5. In the final phase of the motion, the boxer delivers one of the possible blows (right hook to the head, right hook to the body, right uppercut).

Execution technique by Mike Tyson

The adversary delivers the jab and right hook. Tyson ducks to the right-forward taking a step to the left-forward with the left foot and weaves to the left under the opponent's right hook. Accelerating body weight, Tyson delivers the right hook to the opponent's head.

DEMPSEY'S DOUBLE SHIFT

Chasing an opponent, when the first «Dempsey's shift» has not allowed to get close to an opponent for a punch, a boxer may perform a «Dempsey's double shift». Dempsey's Double shift is sequential steps with a bob and weave technique and a constant threat of a punch. The technique is as follows:

1.   A boxer ducks bending the body to the left-forward, transferring the body weight on the left leg.

2.   At the same time, the right foot slides forward, and a boxer switches to the right-side stance.

3.   The body structure charges to the left-hand blow.

4.   A boxer weaves to the right-forward, transferring the body weight on the right leg.

5.   At the same time, the left foot slides forward.

6.   The body structure charges to the right-hand blow.

Also, «Dempsey's double shift» can start in reverse sequence. The technique is as follows.

1. A boxer ducks bending the body to the right-forward, transferring the body weight on the right leg.

2. At the same time, the left foot slides forward.

3. The body structure charges to the right-hand blow.

4. A boxer weaves to the left-forward, transferring the body weight on the left leg.

5. At the same time, the right foot slides forward.

6. The body structure charges to the left-hand blow.

THE FALLING STEP

THE FALLING STEP WITH THE LEFT FOOT

We have already written about the falling step technique more than once, almost in every book. For a complete analysis of peekaboo footwork, we will consider the falling step in this book.

The falling step uses the force of gravity. The falling step technique was firstly described by Jack Dempsey and was later used by Cus D'Amato in creating the peekaboo style. So, the technique of the falling step consists of the following:

1. A boxer is in an orthodox stance, knees slightly bent, the right (rear) foot is on the toe, and almost all the weight is on the left (lead) foot.

2. A boxer pushes off with his right foot and simultaneously takes a step forward with his left foot.

3. Under the action of gravity, a boxer lands on his left foot and moves forward.

4. The right foot is pulled to the left foot.

The basic «falling step» is performed without any transfer of body weight to the rear foot or other preparatory movements. Gravity gives the body a moment of free fall. The step itself can vary in length from long to short. The point is to use the force of gravity to shift and blow.

SECTION 5. THE FALLING STEP

Blows by the falling step with the left foot

The falling step technique is suitable for all kinds of blows (jab, right straight, right cross, right hook, right uppercut). When landing, the right-handed blows like a right cross or a right hook, the boxer takes the falling step with the left foot to the left-forward. In this case, our body will spontaneously slip to the left. This is predetermined by biomechanics. The left slip additionally speeds up the body mass and thereby strengthens a punch. In addition, the left slip shifts the boxer from the line of attack which is an additional protective element. Below are examples of the right blows with the falling step.

Execution by Mike Tyson

Below is the right straight with the falling step. Tyson, pushing off with the right foot from the base stance, takes the falling step to the left-forward with the left foot and delivers the right straight punch, transferring the body weight to the left leg.

THE FALLING STEP WITH THE RIGHT FOOT

The technique of the falling step with the right foot is as follows:

1.   The boxer is in an orthodox stance, knees slightly bent, the right (back) foot is on the toe, and almost all the weight is on the left (front) foot.

2.   The boxer takes a step to the right-forward with his right foot and at the same time pushes off with the left foot.

3.   The body slips to the right, strengthening and accelerating the shift to the right-forward.

4.   Under the influence of gravity, a boxer lands on his right foot and shifts to the right-forward.

Taking the falling step to the right-forward, our body will spontaneously slip to the right. This is predetermined by biomechanics. The right slip speeds up the movement, speeds up the body mass, and thereby strengthens a punch. In addition, the right slip shifts a boxer from the line of attack which is an additional protective element.

Blows by the falling step with the right foot

The falling step to the right-forward technique is suitable for all kinds of left-handed blows (straight, cross, overhand, hook, uppercut). Below are examples of the left blows with the falling step.

SECTION 5. THE FALLING STEP

Biomechanics of the falling step

In terms of biomechanics, before the beginning of the falling step, the projection of the body center is directly on the lead left leg and is practically ready to go beyond the support area. It is this position of the body center ensures a free fall. A boxer then pushes off with his right foot and steps left-forward with his left foot.

A similar thing happens if a boxer takes the falling step to the right-forward with the right foot. Before the falling step, the center of a boxer's body is directly on the lead left leg. A push with the left foot causes the projection of the body center to move beyond the support area and a boxer goes into a free fall.

The balance of forces acting on a boxer gives him a free fall. The force of gravity begins to act. A boxer falls forward and puts his foot forward at the last moment.

THE SHUFFLE FORWARD

The «shuffle forward» can be considered as a basic leap in boxing. With this leap, there is no change of stance or angle of attack. But thanks to this leap, a boxer can quickly approach an opponent, gain speed and accelerate the body mass. In addition, this technique is the basis for other types of «shuffle» leaps (a shuffle to the right, a shuffle to the left, a shuffle-twist to the right, a shuffle-twist to the left).

BASIC TECHNIQUE

The «shuffle forward» is done from a basic stance or with a preliminary step forward with the left foot. Let's consider these options.

1. A boxer is in an orthodox stance.

2. A boxer transfers body weight to the lead left leg.

3. A boxer pushes off with his left foot, simultaneously undercutting his left foot from behind with his right foot.

4. A boxer jumps up and forward, throwing his left foot forward.

5. The whole body moves forward during the jump.

6. A boxer lands on his right foot and throws his left foot forward. At the final position, the left foot is placed forward and the body weight is shifted to the right foot.

If an opponent is at a long distance, a boxer may take a preliminary step forward with his left foot.

1. A boxer takes a step forward with his left foot from a basic stance and transfers his body weight to it. The left leg charges and becomes a pushing one.

2. A boxer pushes off with his left foot, simultaneously undercutting his left foot from behind with his right foot.

3. A boxer leaps up and forward, throwing his left foot forward.

4. The whole body moves forward during the jump.

5. A boxer lands on his right foot and throws his left foot forward. At the final position, the left foot is placed forward and the body weight is shifted to the right foot.

Execution by Mike Tyson

With this leap, Tyson solved the problem of a quick approach to a tall opponent from a long distance. The shuffle forward combines well with the step forward of the lead left foot. The such combination increases the range of the leap. Tyson takes a step forward with his left foot and transfers his weight to it. Then he pushes with his left foot and throws it forward. Simultaneously, the rear right foot undercuts the left foot from behind. The boxer lands on his right foot. All movements are merged and performed as one technical move.

SECTION 6. THE SHUFFLE FORWARD

DEFENSE BY THE SHUFLLE FORWARD

When performing a shuffle forward to get close to an opponent without punching, the opponent may attack. Therefore, the boxer may perform one of the defensive techniques when landing – a slip to the left, a slip to the right, a bob and weave to the left, or a bob and weave to the right. Consider these options.

The shuffle forward slipping to the left

1. The boxer performs the «shuffle forward».
2. The opponent throws a jab.
3. While landing, the boxer slips to the left.

The shuffle forward slipping to the right

1. The boxer performs the «shuffle forward».

2. The opponent throws a jab.

3. While landing, the boxer slips to the right.

Feature. This technique allows a boxer to get close to the opponent, pursue him, and simultaneously get out of the line of attack.

Execution by Mike Tyson

Tyson pursues his opponent and approaches him using «shuffle forward» leaps. After the first «shuffle forward», Tyson slips to his right.

After the second «shuffle forward» leap, Tyson slips to his left.

After the third «shuffle forward», Tyson slips to his right.

The shuffle forward with bobbing and weaving to the right

1. The boxer performs the «shuffle forward».

2. The opponent throws the left hook to the head.

3. While landing, the boxer bobs and weaves to the right, diving under the opponent's hook.

SECTION 6. THE SHUFFLE FORWARD

The shuffle forward with bobbing and weaving to the left

1. The boxer performs the «shuffle forward».

2. The opponent throws the right hook to the head.

3. While landing, the boxer bobs and weaves to the left, diving under the opponent's hook.

Execution by Jose Torres

Torrez comes in close to his opponent, using the «shuffle forward». Immediately after landing, he ducks to his right, dodging his opponent's jab and weaves to the left. Torrez finds himself in close range with a strong punching structure, charged with a left-hand blow.

ATTACKS BY THE SHUFFLE FORWARD

The «shuffle forward» technique is used for a rapid attack or counterattack. In most cases, the main blow in the series is the blow with the right hand after landing. When landing, the body weight is shifted to the right leg and the whole body gains good speed during the leap. As a result, the whole body is charged for the right hand punch. Therefore, the right punch is heavy, powerful and often a knockout punch.

The main combination using the leap «shuffle forward» is a series of two punches «jab – right punch». The right blow may be anything – straight, cross, hook, overhand, uppercut. The blows are delivered immediately, one after the other, on a «one-two» count.

Possible blows with the right hand after performing the «shuffle forward» are shown below:

Combination

1. The boxer takes a step forward with his left foot from a basic stance and performs the "shuffle forward".

2. Leaping forward, the boxer throws the left jab to the opponent's head.

3. Immediately after landing, the boxer delivers the right hook to the opponent's head, leaning to the left and transferring weight to his left leg.

Execution by Mike Tyson

Tyson takes a small step forward with his left foot, then performs the «shuffle forward» throwing the jab to the opponent's head. The body mass speeds up. After landing on the right foot, the left foot is brought forward. As a result, Tyson takes a strong punching structure with his body weight transferred to his right leg. Immediately after landing, Tyson lands the powerful right hook to the opponent's head, transferring body weight to the left leg.

THE SHUFFLE TO THE LEFT

The next peekaboo footwork technique, which changes the boxer's position relative to an opponent, is performed by «the shuffle to the left». The shuffle to the left is a type of leap where a boxer pushes with the left foot and lands on the right foot, turning to the left and switching the stance to a southpaw. A boxer can perform this kind of leap from the basic stance, from a preliminary slip to the left, with a preliminary step to the left, or to the left-forward with the left foot. From these positions, it is biomechanically convenient to perform a «shuffle to the left».

Some boxing researchers call this type of footwork the "southpaw reset", focusing on the fact that the boxer takes a left-handed stance after the leap. Other researchers call this futhering technique the D'Amato shift, emphasizing that this technique is used in peekaboo and was developed and implemented by Cus D'Amato.

BASIC TECHNIQUE

1. A boxer transfers body weight to the lead left leg.

2. A boxer pushes off with his left foot, simultaneously undercutting his left foot from behind with his right foot.

3. A boxer leaps to the left-forward, throwing his left foot to the left and simultaneously turning his body clockwise to the right.

4. A boxer lands on his right foot. At the final position, the right foot is placed forward and the body weight is shifted to the right foot.

Feature. The leap is used at close and medium distances.

Execution by Mike Tyson

In the photos below, from the frontal stance, Mike Tyson transfers his body weight to his left leg and pushes off with it. After the push, the left foot is thrown to the left and the right foot is put in place of the left one. The body turns clockwise (to the right) during the leap. When landing, body weight is shifted to the right leg, the right side of the body is loaded for a blow.

A slip to the left – a shuffle to the left

To strengthen the leap, a boxer can previously transfer the body weight to the left leg slipping to the left. The left leg is charged and becomes the pushing leg. From this position, a boxer performs the shuffle to the left. As a result, the leap is performed according to the scheme «a slip to the left – a shuffle to the left».

SECTION 7. THE SHUFFLE TO THE LEFT

If a boxer is at a long range, the «shuffle to the left» can be performed with a preliminary step to the left-forward with the left foot. The consistent technique for this footwork maneuver is as follows:

1. A boxer takes a step to the left-forward (or to the left) with the left foot and slips to the left, transferring body weight to the lead left leg.

2. A boxer pushes off with his left foot, simultaneously undercutting his left foot from behind with his right foot.

3. A boxer leaps to the left-forward, throwing his left foot to the left and simultaneously turning his body clockwise to the right.

4. A boxer lands on his right foot. At the final position, the right foot is placed forward, and the body weight is shifted to the right foot.

Feature. This variation of the leap «shuffle to the left» can be used to get close to an opponent from medium to close range.

SWITCHING THE STANCE AND ANGLE OF ATTACK

Using the «shuffle to the left», the boxer can switch his stance and change the angle of attack. By leaping, the boxer moves to the left relative to the opponent, approaches the opponent from the left flank, and switches from the orthodox stance to the southpaw stance. After landing, the right foot is in front, the body weight is on the right foot, and the body structure is charged to punch with the right hand.

The diagram of the leap is shown below. A boxer moves to the left and switches his stance from the orthodox to the southpaw. Most of the body weight is on the lead right leg after the leap.

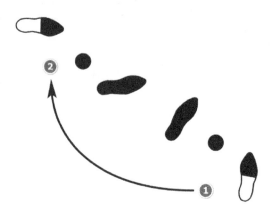

Execution by Mike Tyson

Below is an example of the «shuffle to the left» with a preliminary step and slip to the left. Tyson steps to the left with the left foot, slipping to the left. From this position, Tyson pushes off with the left foot, undercuts the left foot with his right foot and throws his left foot to the left. The body turns clockwise to the right. Tyson lands on the right foot and so switches his stance to a southpaw stance.

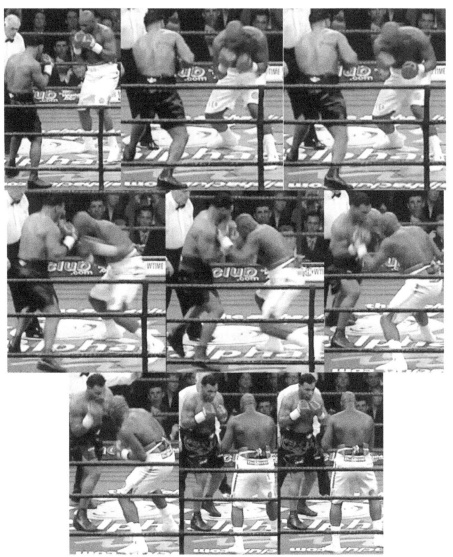

DEFENSE BY THE SHUFFLE TO THE LEFT

The technique can be used to defend against straight blows with both left and right hands.

1. The opponent throws the right straight punch.
2. The boxer takes a step to the left with his left foot, slipping to the left.
3. The boxer performs the «shuffle to the left».

SECTION 7. THE SHUFFLE TO THE LEFT

Execution by Mike Tyson

An example of defense by the «shuffle to the left» is shown in the photos below. The opponent lands a right straight to the head. Tyson takes a short step with his left foot to the left slipping to the left. After that, Tyson quickly uses the «shuffle to the left» to switch a stance to the southpaw and to change the angle of attack.

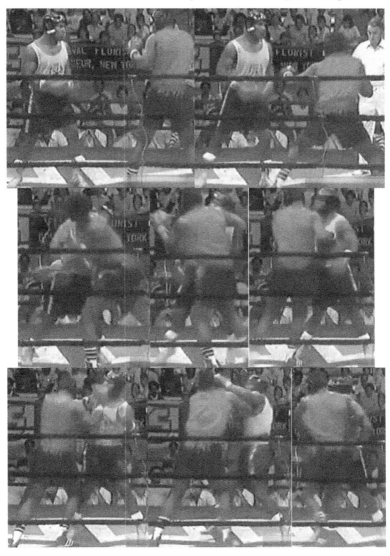

ATTACKS BY THE SHUFFLE TO THE LEFT

PREPARATORY BLOWS BEFORE THE LEAP

The «shuffle to the left» may be preceded by preparatory blows. These blows create the biomechanical conditions for the leap. Basically, these are blows with the right hand, transferring the body weight to the left leg. This fully loads the left leg with the weight and the left foot becomes the pushing one. A powerful push with the left foot allows executing the «shuffle to the left».

Also as preparatory blows may be blows with the left hand, after which a boxer slips to the left. For example, a left jab, left uppercut, left hook to the body with a subsequent left slip.

Besides, these blows hide a boxer's tactical intention to leap by distracting an opponent's attention. Preparatory blows often force an opponent to cover up. At this point, a boxer disappears from view. Therefore, it is possible to cut the angle and move to the left unnoticed.

SECTION 7. THE SHUFFLE TO THE LEFT

Right-hand blows before leaping

1. The boxer delivers the right straight to the head (or the right straight to the body or the right hook to the head) using the falling step with the left foot to the left-forward.

2. The boxer performs the «shuffle to the left».

Left-hand blows before leaping

1. The boxer delivers a jab using the falling step with the left foot to the left-forward from a long distance.

1a. The boxer delivers a left hook to the body or a left uppercut at close range.

2. After the blow, the boxer slips to his left.

3. The boxer performs the «shuffle to the left».

SINGLE BLOWS WITH THE LEAP

During the leap to the left, a boxer can throw a blow with the left hand. These types of blows are not knockout blows, but they allow a boxer to hide the beginning of the leap and distract the opponent's attention.

1. The boxer takes a step with his left foot to the left-forward (or to the left) and performs the «shuffle to the left».

2. Leaping to the left, the boxer delivers one of the possible blows with the left hand – a left straight, a left hook, or a left uppercut to the opponent's head.

Execution by Mike Tyson

At close range, Tyson takes the shuffle to the left and simultaneously throws the left hook to the body. Leaping, Tyson switches the stance to the southpaw and turns clockwise to the right. When landing, the body weight is shifted to the right foot and the right hand is charged for the punch.

BLOWS AFTER THE LEAP

In most cases, the main punch is a right hand punch after leaping and landing. When landing, the body weight is transferred to the right foot, the body turns to the right, so the entire body is charged with the right blow. The stance is strong and stable, the center of the body does not go beyond the support area. Therefore, the right punch will be heavy, powerful, and often a knockout blow. After leaping, the boxer can deliver a right uppercut to the head, a right hook to the head, a right hook to the body.

The shuffle to the left – the right hook to the head

1. The boxer steps to the left-forward (or to the left) with the left foot, slipping to the left and then takes the shuffle to the left.

2. Immediately after landing, the boxer delivers the right hook or the leaping right hook to the opponent's head.

SECTION 7. THE SHUFFLE TO THE LEFT

Execution by Mike Tyson

At the middle range, Tyson steps to the left with the left foot, slipping to the left and then takes the shuffle to the left. When landing, the body weight is shifted to the right foot and the right hand is charged for the punch. Immediately after landing, the boxer delivers the right leaping hook to the opponent's head.

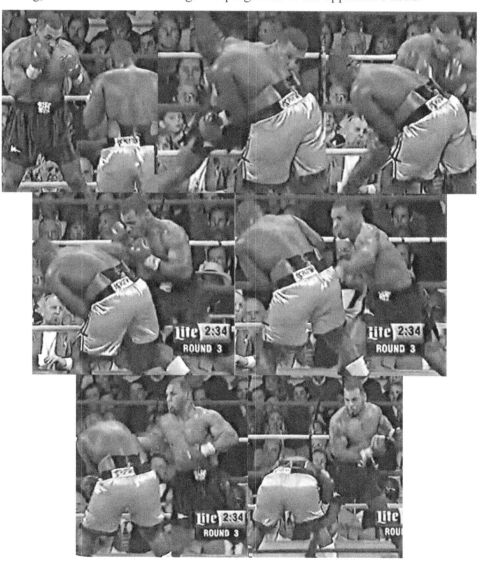

PUNCHING COMBINATIONS AFTER LANDING

Immediately after landing, the boxer can attack the opponent not only with a single blow but with one of the possible peekaboo punching combinations. Consider them in order.

The shuffle to the left – the right uppercut to the head – the right uppercut to the head

1. The boxer performs the «shuffle to the left».

2. Immediately after landing, the boxer delivers the punching series «the right uppercut to the head – the right uppercut to the head», keeping the weight on the right leg.

The shuffle to the left – the right hook to the body – the right uppercut to the head

1. The boxer performs the «shuffle to the left».

2. Immediately after landing, the boxer delivers the punching series «the right hook to the body – the right uppercut to the head», keeping the weight on the right leg.

The shuffle to the left – the right uppercut to the head – the left cross to the head

1. The boxer performs the «shuffle to the left».

2. Immediately after landing, the boxer delivers the punching series «the right uppercut to the head – the left cross to the head».

SECTION 7. THE SHUFFLE TO THE LEFT

Execution by Mike Tyson

At close range, Tyson steps to the left with the left foot, slipping to the left, and then switches the stance to the southpaw using the shuffle to the left. When landing, the body weight is shifted to the right foot and Tyson charges the right side of body for the punch. Immediately after landing, Tyson delivers a punching series the right uppercut to the head – the left cross to the head».

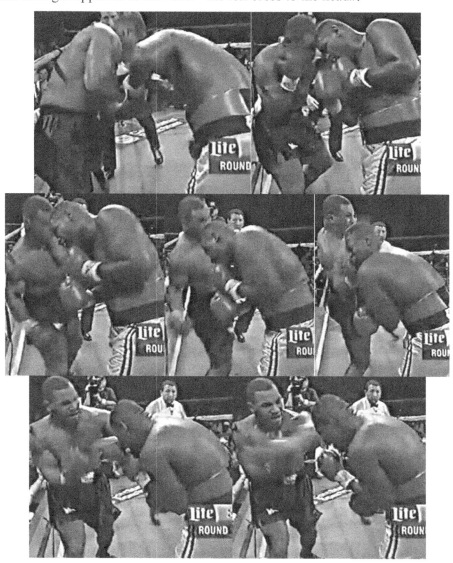

COMBINATORICS OF PUNCHING COMBINATIONS

So, when using the shuffle to the left, blows can be delivered at any stage in combinational boxing peekaboo:

1. Blows before the shuffle to the left (both single and series).

2. Blows with the shuffle to the left with the left hand.

3. Blows after the shuffle to the left (both singles and series).

The most complete punching combinations will be series using blows before the shuffle to the left, blows with the shuffle to the left, and blows after landing (in a total of 3 to 7 punches). The shortest punching combination will be a combination with a single blow after landing. The blows can be different and in different combinations. From this comes the punch combinatorics. Let's consider an example of building a multi-punch combination, using the shuffle to the left.

1. The boxer takes the falling step with the left foot to the left-forward and delivers the right punch to the opponent's body.

2. The boxer performs the «shuffle to the left», throwing the left hook and switching the stance to the southpaw.

SECTION 7. THE SHUFFLE TO THE LEFT

3.   Immediately after landing, the boxer delivers the punching series «the right uppercut to the head – the right uppercut to the head».

Similarly, it is possible to combine other punch combinations based on the leap «shuffle to the left». The main requirements for composing a punching series are:

–   economy of motion – the punch series should not be overloaded with a large number of blows.

–   biomechanical basis for the blows – include in the series only those blows that arise from the biomechanics of the movement. The blows should be easy to perform and have maximum force.

–   blows to different levels – alternate blows to the head and to the body between each other.

Combination

1. The boxer takes the falling step with the left foot to the left-forward and delivers the right punch to the opponent's head.

2. The boxer performs the «shuffle to the left».

3. Immediately after landing, the boxer delivers the punching series «the right hook to the body – the right uppercut to the head».

SECTION 7. THE SHUFFLE TO THE LEFT

Combination

1. The boxer delivers a jab using the falling step with the left foot to the left-forward and then slips to the left.

2. The boxer performs the «shuffle to the left», switching the stance to the southpaw.

3. Immediately after landing, the boxer delivers the punching series «the right hook to the head – the left cross to the head».

Execution by Mike Tyson

At the middle range, Tyson steps to the left-forward with the left foot, throwing the jab. Then Tyson slips to the left. The body weight shifts to the left leg. From this position, Tyson switches the stance from orthodox to southpaw using the leap "shuffle to the left". When landing, the body weight is on the right foot and the right hand is charged for the punch. Immediately after landing, Tyson delivers a punching series: the right leaping hook to the head – the left cross to the head.

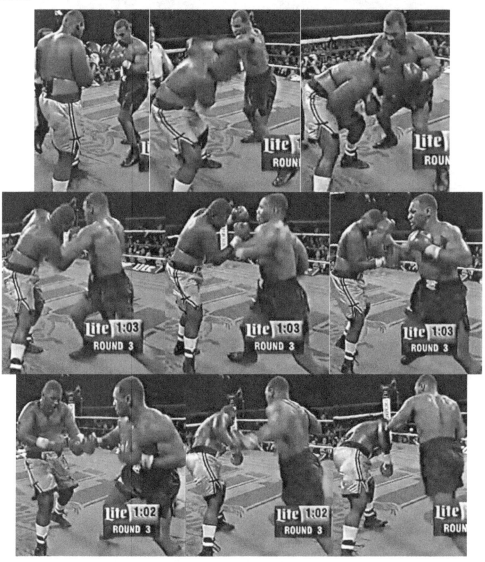

SECTION 7. THE SHUFFLE TO THE LEFT

Combination

1. The boxer throws a jab, stepping to the left-forward with his left foot.

2. The boxer slips to the left and shifts his body weight to his left leg.

3. Next, the boxer performs the shuffle to the left, switching his stance to the southpaw stance and taking the charged position for a right blow.

4. From this position, the boxer delivers the right uppercut to the opponent's head jumping up.

Execution by Mike Tyson

The fight «Mike Tyson – Julius Francis» demonstrates the switch of stance technique by using the leap "shuffle to the left". Tyson throws the feint jab, stepping to the left-forward with the left foot.

Next, he uses the shuffle to the left. Leaping, Tyson throws his left foot to the left and turns his body clockwise to the right. Then he lands in the southpaw stance with his body weight on his right leg. From this position, Tyson delivers the right uppercut to the body.

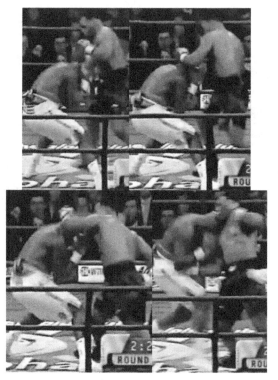

SECTION 7. THE SHUFFLE TO THE LEFT

Combination

1. The boxer throws a jab, stepping to the left-forward with his left foot.

2. The boxer slips to the left and shifts his body weight to his left leg.

3. Next, the boxer performs the shuffle to the left, switching his stance to the southpaw and taking the charged position for a right blow.

4. From this position, the boxer delivers the leaping right hook to the opponent's head.

Execution by Mike Tyson

Stepping to the left-forward with the left foot Tyson throws the jab.

Then, Tyson slips to his left shifting his body weight to his left leg. From the left slipping position, Tyson switches the stance to the southpaw using the shuffle to the left. When landing, the body weight is on the right foot. The right side of the body is loaded for a blow.

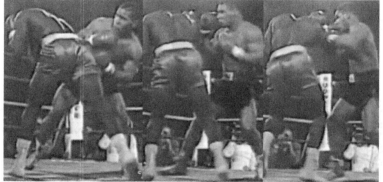

From this position, Tyson pushes off and lands the leaping right hook to the opponent's head.

Combination

1. The boxer delivers the left hook, taking a side-step to the left-forward with his left foot and slips to the left, shifting his body weight to his left leg.

2. The boxer performs the shuffle to the left, switching his stance to the southpaw.

3.   From this position, the boxer delivers two leaping right hooks to the opponent's head.

Execution by Mike Tyson

Tyson attacks from long range. He takes a side-step to the left-forward with the left foot, simultaneously delivering the left hook to the opponent's head. Immediately after the left hook, Tyson slips to his left, shifting his body weight to the left leg. From this position, Tyson changes his stance using the shuffle to the left. Tyson finds himself in a southpaw stance (a right foot and a right hand in front).

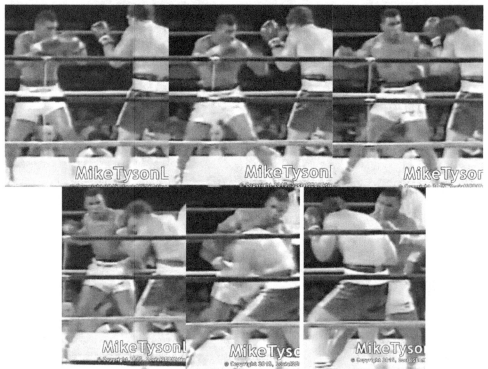

After switching the stance, Tyson delivers two consecutive leaping right hooks to the opponent's head from the southpaw stance.

Combination

1. At close range, the boxer slips to the left.

2. The boxer delivers the left hook to the opponent's body, performing the shuffle to the left.

3. Under landing, the boxer turns clockwise to the right, switching the stance to the southpaw.

4. Immediately after landing, the boxer delivers the right uppercut to the opponent's head.

Execution by Mike Tyson

At close range, Tyson takes the shuffle to the left and simultaneously throws the left hook to the body. Leaping, Tyson switches the stance to the southpaw and turns clockwise to the right. When landing, the body weight is shifted to the right foot and the right hand is charged for the punch. Immediately after landing, Tyson delivers the right uppercut to the opponent's head.

THE SHUFFLE TO THE RIGHT

The next technique of peekaboo footwork is a «shuffle to the right». The shuffle to the right is a type of leap where a boxer pushes with the right foot and lands on the left foot, turning to the left and moving to the right. There is no change of stance to a southpaw after this leap. However, the boxer changes the angle of attack, moves to the right flank, and attacks from the new position.

A boxer can perform this kind of leap from the basic stance, from a preliminary slip to the right, with a preliminary step to the right, or to the right-forward with the right foot. These positions create the biomechanical conditions for the «shuffle to the right» leap.

BASIC TECHNIQUE

1. A boxer transfers body weight to the rear right leg.

2. A boxer pushes off with his right foot, simultaneously undercutting his right foot from the left with his left foot.

3. A boxer leaps to the right-forward, throws his right foot to the right, simultaneously turning his body counterclockwise to the left.

4. A boxer lands on his left foot. At the final position, the left foot is placed forward, and the body weight is shifted to the left foot.

Feature. The leap is used at close and medium distances.

Execution by Mike Tyson

In the photos below, from the frontal stance, Mike Tyson transfers his body weight to his right leg and pushes off with it. After the push, the right foot is thrown to the right and the left foot is put in place of the right one. The body turns counterclockwise (to the left) during the leap. When landing, body weight is shifted to the left leg, and the left side of the body is loaded for a blow.

SECTION 8. THE SHUFFLE TO THE RIGHT

A slip to the right – a shuffle to the right

To strengthen the leap, a boxer can previously transfer the body weight to the right leg by slipping to the right. The right leg is charged and becomes the pushing one. As a result, the leap is performed according to the scheme «a slip to the right – a shuffle to the right».

Execution by Mike Tyson

The opponent from long range delivers the left leaping hook. Tyson takes a step to the right with his right foot, ducking to the right. The body weight is transferred to the right foot. Next, the boxer takes the shuffle to the right. Landing on his left foot after the leap, his body weight is on his left foot.

If a boxer is at a long range, the leap «shuffle to the right» can be performed with a preliminary step to the right or right-forward with the right foot. The consistent technique for this footwork maneuver is as follows:

1.   A boxer takes a step to the right-forward (or to the right) with the right foot and slips to the right, transferring body weight to the right leg.

2.   A boxer pushes off with his right foot, simultaneously undercutting his right foot from the left with his left foot.

3.   A boxer leaps to the right-forward, throws his right foot to the right, simultaneously turning his body counterclockwise to the left.

4.   A boxer lands on his left foot. At the final position, the left foot is placed forward, and the body weight is shifted to the left foot.

Feature. This variation of the leap «shuffle to the right» can be used to get close to an opponent from long to close range.

Execution by Mike Tyson

Tyson, being at close range, takes a step to the right with his right foot and slips to the right, transferring body weight to the right leg. From this position, Tyson takes the shuffle to the right. After landing, the body weight is transferred to the left leg, and the left side of the body is charged for a blow with the left hand.

SWITCHING THE STANCE AND ANGLE OF ATTACK

The «shuffle to the right» does not lead to a switch of stance. A boxer only changes a stance relatively to an opponent but stays in **a left-side stance**. By leaping, the boxer moves to the right relative to the opponent, approaches the opponent from the right flank, cuts an angle, and changes the angle of attack. After landing, the boxer is in an orthodox stance with the body weight on the lead left leg and the body structure is charged to punch with the left hand.

The diagram of the leap is shown below. A boxer moves to the right without switching stance and stays in the orthodox stance. Most of the body weight is on the lead left leg after the leap.

DEFENSE BY THE SHUFFLE TO THE RIGHT

The technique can be used to defend against straight blows with both left and right hands.

1. The opponent throws a jab.
2. The boxer takes a step to the right with his right foot, slipping to the right.
3. The boxer performs the «shuffle to the right».

ATTACKS BY THE SHUFFLE TO THE RIGHT

PREPARATORY BLOWS BEFORE THE LEAP

The «shuffle to the right" may be preceded by blows. These blows create the biomechanical conditions for the leap. Basically, these are the left-hand blows using the falling step with the right foot to the right-forward. These blows fully load the right leg with the weight and the right foot becomes the pushing one. A powerful push with the right foot allows making the «shuffle to the right».

To strengthen this type of blows, it is advisable to slip preliminary to the left, charging the left leg for the subsequent push.

The left straight to the head before leaping to the right

1. The boxer delivers the left straight to the opponent's head using the falling step to the right-forward with the right foot

2. The boxer performs the «shuffle to the right».

Execution by Mike Tyson

Tyson throws a straight left to the opponent's head taking the falling step with the right foot to the right. Body weight is transferred to the right leg and the fighter takes the shuffle to the right. On landing, body weight is shifted to the left leg. The left side of the body is charged to punch.

SECTION 8. THE SHUFFLE TO THE RIGHT

Similarly, before the leap, other left-hand blows can be applied using the falling step to the right-forward with the right foot – the left straight to the body, the left hook to the opponent's head.

SINGLE BLOWS WITH THE LEAP

Leaping to the right, it is possible to throw blows with the right hand. These types of blows are not knockout blows, but they allow a boxer to hide the beginning of the leap and distract the opponent's attention.

1. The boxer takes a step to the right-forward with his right foot (or to the right) and performs the «shuffle to the right».

2. Leaping to the right, the boxer delivers one of the possible blows with the right blow – a right straight, a right hook or a right uppercut to the head.

SECTION 8. THE SHUFFLE TO THE RIGHT

Combination

1.   The boxer takes a step to the right-forward with his right foot.

2.   The boxer performs the «shuffle to the right».

3.   Leaping to the right, the boxer delivers the right cross to the opponent's head.

Execution by Mike Tyson

In the course of the fight, Tyson finds himself with his left side to his opponent, in an unfavorable tactical position. For a quick turnaround, Tyson performs the shuffle to the right, jumping up and turning his body counterclockwise. Leaping counterclockwise, Tyson lands the right straight to the opponent's head. His opponent is knocked out.

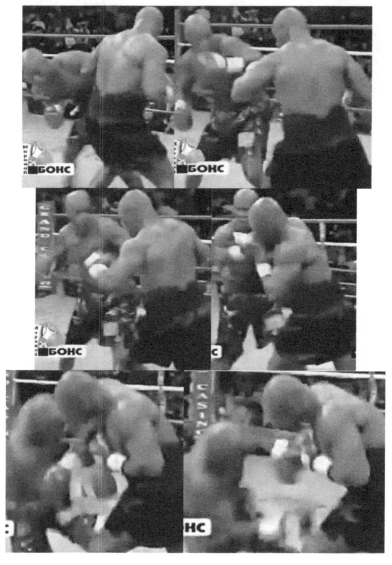

BLOWS AFTER THE LEAP

This footwork technique can be used to attack and counterattack. In most cases, the main punch is a left hand punch after leaping and landing. When landing, the body weight is transferred to the left foot, so the entire body is charged with the left blow. The stance is strong and stable, the center of the body does not go beyond the support area. Therefore, the left punch will be heavy, powerful, and often a knockout blow. After leaping, the boxer can deliver a left uppercut to the head, a left hook to the head, a left hook to the body.

The shuffle to the right – the left hook to the head

1. The boxer takes a step to the right with his right foot.

2. The boxer performs the «shuffle to the right».

3. Immediately after landing, the boxer delivers the left leaping hook to the opponent's head.

Execution by Mike Tyson

The opponent from long range delivers the left leaping hook. Tyson takes a step to the right with his right foot, ducking to the right. The body weight is transferred to the right foot. Next, the boxer takes the shuffle to the right. Landing on his left foot after the leap, his body weight is on his left foot, the left side of the body is charged with a blow. Immediately after landing, Tyson delivers the left leaping hook.

PUNCHING COMBINATIONS AFTER LANDING

Immediately after landing, the boxer can attack the opponent not only with a single blow but with one of the possible peekaboo punching combinations. Consider them in order.

The shuffle to the right – the left uppercut to the head – the left uppercut to the head

1. The boxer performs the «shuffle to the right».

2. Immediately after landing, the boxer delivers the punching series «the left uppercut to the head – the left uppercut to the head», keeping the weight on the left leg.

The shuffle to the right – the left hook to the body – the left uppercut to the head

1. The boxer performs the «shuffle to the right».

2. Immediately after landing, the boxer delivers the punching series «the left hook to the body – the left uppercut to the head», keeping the weight on the left leg.

The shuffle to the right – the left uppercut to the head – the right cross to the head

1. The boxer performs the «shuffle to the right».

2. Immediately after landing, the boxer delivers the punching series «the left uppercut to the head – the right cross to the head».

Execution by Mike Tyson

At close range, Tyson switches the stance to the southpaw using the shuffle to the right. When landing, the body weight is shifted to the left foot and the body is charged for the left punch. Immediately after landing, Tyson delivers the punching series «the left uppercut to the head – the right cross to the head».

COMBINATORICS OF PUNCHING COMBINATIONS

So, when using the shuffle to the right, blows can be delivered at any stage in combinational boxing peekaboo:

1. Blows before the shuffle to the right (both single and series).
2. Blows with the shuffle to the right with the right hand.
3. Blows after the shuffle to the right (both singles and series).

The most complete punching combinations will be series using blows before the shuffle to the right, blows with the shuffle to the right, and blows after landing (in a total of 3 to 7 punches). The shortest punching combination will be a combination with a single blow after landing. The blows can be different and in different combinations. From this comes the punch combinatorics. Let's consider an example of building a multi-punch combination, using the shuffle to the right.

1. The boxer takes the falling step to the right-forward with the right foot, delivering the left punch to the opponent's body.

2. The boxer performs the «shuffle to the right».

3.   Immediately after landing, the boxer delivers the punching series «the left hook to the body – the left uppercut to the head».

Similarly, it is possible to combine other punch combinations based on the leap «shuffle to the right». The main requirements for composing a punching series are:

–   economy of motion – the punch series should not be overloaded with a large number of blows.

–   biomechanical basis for the blows – include in the series only those blows that arise from the biomechanics of the movement. The blows should be easy to perform and have maximum force.

–   blows to different levels – alternate blows to the head and to the body between each other.

Combination

1. The boxer takes the falling step to the right-forward with the right foot, delivering the left punch to the opponent's head.

2. The boxer performs the «shuffle to the right».

3. Immediately after landing, the boxer delivers the punching series «the left uppercut to the head – the left uppercut to the head», keeping the weight on the left leg.

SECTION 8. THE SHUFFLE TO THE RIGHT

Execution by Mike Tyson

Tyson takes a step to the right-forward with his right foot, delivering the left punch to the opponent's head.

The body weight is transferred to the right leg. Tyson performs the shuffle to the right. Under landing, the body weight is on the left leg and the body is charged with the left-hand blow.

Immediately after landing, the boxer delivers two left uppercuts, keeping the body weight on the left leg.

Combination

1. The boxer takes the falling step to the right-forward with the right foot, delivering the left punch to the opponent's head.

2. The boxer performs the «shuffle to the right».

3. Immediately after landing, the boxer delivers the punching series «the left uppercut to the head – the right cross to the head».

SECTION 8. THE SHUFFLE TO THE RIGHT

Combination

1. The boxer slips to the left and shifts his body weight to his left leg.

2. The boxer takes the falling step to the right-forward with the right foot, delivering the left hook to the opponent's head.

3. The boxer performs the «shuffle to the right».

4. Immediately after landing, the boxer delivers the punching series «the left uppercut to the head – the right uppercut to the body», keeping the weight on the left leg.

Combination

1. The boxer slips to the left and shifts his body weight to his left leg.

2. The boxer takes the falling step to the right-forward with the right foot, delivering the left hook to the opponent's head.

3. The boxer performs the «shuffle to the right».

4. Immediately after landing, the boxer delivers the punching series «the left hook to the body – the left uppercut to the head», keeping the weight on the left leg.

Combination

1. The boxer slips to the left and shifts his body weight to his left leg.

2. The boxer takes the falling step to the right-forward with the right foot, delivering the left hook to the opponent's head.

3. The boxer performs the «shuffle to the right».

4. Immediately after landing, the boxer delivers the punching series «the left uppercut to the head – the right cross to the head».

THE SHUFFLE-TWIST TO THE LEFT

The next footwork trick is the «shuffle-twist to the left» (clockwise). This is based on the «shuffle forward» leap, but also adds a clockwise twist of the whole body. The shuffle-twist to the left is a type of leap where a boxer pushes with the left foot and lands on the right foot, simultaneously twisting clockwise and moving to the left-forward. This type of leap can be done from a basic stance, from a preliminary slip to the left and with a preliminary step to the left-forward with the left foot.

BASIC TECHNIQUE

1. A boxer transfers body weight to the lead left leg. The left leg is charged and becomes a pushing one.

2. A boxer pushes off with his left foot, simultaneously undercutting his left foot from behind with his right foot.

3. A boxer leaps forward, throwing his left foot forward and simultaneously twisting his body clockwise to the right.

4. A boxer lands on his right foot. At the final position, the left foot is placed forward and the body weight is shifted to the right foot.

Feature. The leap is used at long and medium distances.

SECTION 9. THE SHUFFLE-TWIST TO THE LEFT

Execution by Kevin Rooney

Kevin Rooney is in a frontal stance. Body weight is evenly distributed on both legs. The boxer transfers his body weight to his left leg and pushes off the ground with it, leaping forward. The right foot undercuts the left foot from behind and the left foot is thrown forward. Simultaneously, the body twists sharply clockwise. The boxer lands on his right foot.

A slip to the left – a shuffle-twist to the left

To strengthen the leap, a boxer can previously transfer the body weight to the left leg slipping to the left. The left leg is charged and becomes the pushing leg. As a result, the leap is performed according to the scheme «a slip to the left – a shuffle-twist to the left».

If a boxer is at a long range, the leap «shuffle-twist to the left» can be performed with a preliminary step to the left-forward with the left foot. The consistent technique for this footwork maneuver is as follows:

1.   A boxer takes a step to the left-forward with the left foot and slips to the left, transferring body weight to the lead left leg.

2.   A boxer pushes off with his left foot, simultaneously undercutting his left foot from behind with his right foot.

3.   A boxer leaps forward, throwing his left foot forward and simultaneously twisting his body clockwise to the right.

4.   A boxer lands on his right foot. At the final position, the left foot is placed forward, and the body weight is shifted to the right foot.

Feature. The leap is used at long distance.

SWITCHING THE STANCE AND ANGLE OF ATTACK

The «shuffle-twist to the left» is used at medium and long range. It does not lead to a switch of stance. But using this leap a boxer can cut an angle and change the angle of attack. By leaping, the boxer moves to the left relative to the opponent, approaches the opponent from the left flank. After landing, the boxer is in an orthodox stance with the body weight on the rear right leg and the body structure is charged to punch with the right hand. The leap allows a boxer to move sharply closer to his opponent, change the angles of attack, and charge his right hand to strike.

The diagram of the leap is shown below. A boxer moves to the left-forward without switching his stance from the orthodox to the southpaw. Most of the body weight is on the rear right leg after leaping.

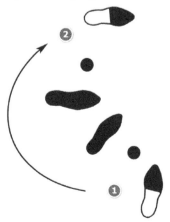

DEFENSE BY THE SHUFFLE-TWIST TO THE LEFT

The technique can be used to defend against straight blows with both left and right hands.

Defense against a jab

1. The opponent throws a jab.

2. The boxer takes a step to the left-forward with his left foot, slipping to the left.

3. The boxer performs the «shuffle-twist to the left» turning clockwise.

Defense against a right straight

1. The opponent throws a right straight punch.

2. The boxer takes a step to the left-forward with his left foot, slipping to the left.

3. The boxer performs the «shuffle-twist to the left» turning clockwise.

Execution by Mike Tyson

An example of defense using the leap «shuffle-twist to the left» is shown in the photos below. The opponent lands a jab to the head. Tyson takes a short step with his left foot to the left-forward slipping to the left. His body weight is shifted to his left foot. The position is comfortable for the shuffle-twist clockwise. After that, Tyson quickly uses a «shuffle- twist to the left» to change the angle of attack.

SECTION 9. THE SHUFFLE-TWIST TO THE LEFT

Defense against a right hook

This footwork tool can be combined with the bob and weave technique. In this case, the maneuver is performed according to the scheme «bob and weave to the left – shuffle-twist to the left».

1. The opponent delivers the right hook.

2. The boxer ducks to the right and then dives sharply under the opponent's left hook, transferring the body weight to the left foot.

3. The boxer pushes with the left foot and performs the «shuffle-twist to the left» turning clockwise.

ATTACKS BY THE SHUFFLE-TWIST TO THE LEFT

PREPARATORY BLOWS BEFORE THE LEAP

Before the «shuffle-twist to the left», a boxer can deliver blows to prepare the leap biomechanically. These blows create the biomechanical conditions for the leap. Basically, these are blows with the right hand, transferring the body weight to the left leg. This fully loads the left leg with the weight and the left foot becomes the pushing one. A powerful push with the left foot allows executing the «shuffle-twist to the left». Besides, these blows hide a boxer's tactical intention to leap by distracting an opponent's attention.

SECTION 9. THE SHUFFLE-TWIST TO THE LEFT

Right-hand blows before leaping

Below are photos of possible right- handed blows before the "shuffle-twist to the left" leap.

1.   The boxer delivers the right straight to the opponent's head (or the right straight to the body or the right hook to the head) using the falling step with the left foot to the left-forward.

2.   The boxer performs the «shuffle-twist to the left».

SINGLE BLOWS WITH THE LEAP

A boxer can throw blows using this leap. The left foot is the pushing foot and a push speeds up the body mass well, which is the basis of a strong blow. The blow can be delivered either powerfully or lightly. In the second case, the blow allows a boxer to divert an opponent's attention to change the angle of attack.

1. The boxer takes a step with his left foot to the left-forward (or to the left) and performs the «shuffle-twist to the left» turning clockwise.

2. Leaping, the boxer delivers one of the possible leaping blows with the left hand – a left straight, a left hook, or a left uppercut to the opponent's head.

Execution by Mike Tyson

At long range, Tyson slips to the left, taking a step to the left-forward with the left foot. Then Tyson takes the shuffle-twist to the left, turning clockwise, and simultaneously throws the left leaping uppercut. When landing, the body weight is shifted to the right foot and the right hand is charged for the punch.

BLOWS AFTER THE LEAP

After the leap, a boxer changes the angle of attack, which can be used to deliver a strong blow. The body weight is shifted to the right leg, so the whole body is charged to strike with the right hand. Immediately after landing, the boxer can deliver one of the possible blows with the right hand – a hook to the head, a hook to the body, a cross to the head.

The shuffle-twist to the left – the right uppercut to the head

1. The boxer steps to the left-forward with the left foot, slipping to the left and then takes the shuffle-twist to the left, turning clockwise.

2. Immediately after landing, the boxer delivers the right uppercut to the opponent's head.

Execution by Mike Tyson

The opponent delivers the right straight at the middle range. Tyson slips to the left and then takes the shuffle-twist to the left, twisting clockwise. So, he moves on the left flank, cutting the angle. When landing, the body weight is shifted to the right foot and the right hand is charged for the punch. Immediately after landing, the boxer delivers the right uppercut to the opponent's head.

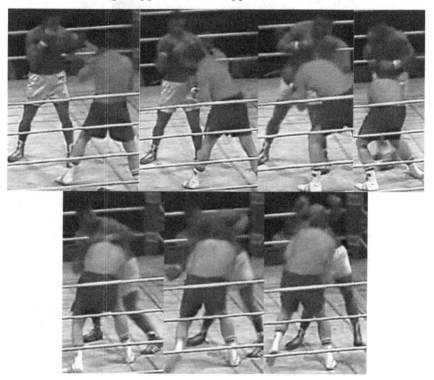

PUNCHING COMBINATIONS AFTER LANDING

Immediately after landing, the boxer can attack the opponent not only with a single blow but with one of the possible peekaboo punching combinations. Consider them in order.

The shuffle-twist to the left – the right uppercut to the head – the right uppercut to the head

1. The boxer performs the «shuffle-twist to the left», twisting clockwise.

2. Immediately after landing, the boxer delivers the punching series «the right uppercut to the head – the right uppercut to the head», keeping the weight on the right leg.

The shuffle-twist to the left – the right hook to the body – the right uppercut to the head

1. The boxer performs the «shuffle-twist to the left», twisting clockwise.

2. Immediately after landing, the boxer delivers the punching series «the right hook to the body – the right uppercut to the head», keeping the weight on the right leg.

SECTION 9. THE SHUFFLE-TWIST TO THE LEFT

The shuffle-twist to the left – the right uppercut to the head – the left cross to the head

1. The boxer performs the «shuffle-twist to the left», twisting clockwise.

2. Immediately after landing, the boxer delivers the punching series «the right uppercut to the head – the left cross to the head».

COMBINATORICS OF PUNCHING COMBINATIONS

So, when using the shuffle-twist to the left, blows can be delivered at any stage in combinational boxing peekaboo:

1. Blows before the shuffle-twist to the left (both single and series).

2. Blows with the shuffle-twist to the left with the left hand.

3. Blows after the shuffle-twist to the left (both singles and series).

The most complete punching combinations will be series using blows before the shuffle-twist to the left, blows with the shuffle-twist to the left, and blows after landing (in a total of 3 to 7 punches). The shortest punching combination will be a combination with a single blow after landing. The blows can be different and in different combinations. From this comes the punch combinatorics. Let's consider an example of building a multi-punch combination, using the shuffle-twist to the left.

1. The boxer throws a punching series "left jab – right cross" to the opponent's head, transferring the body weight to the left leg.

2.   The boxer performs the «shuffle-twist to the left», throwing the left leaping hook and twisting clockwise.

3.   Immediately after landing, the boxer delivers the punching series «the right uppercut to the head – the right uppercut to the head».

Similarly, it is possible to combine other punch combinations based on the leap «shuffle-twist to the left». The main requirements for composing a punching series are:

–   economy of motion – the punch series should not be overloaded with a large number of blows.

–   biomechanical basis for the blows – include in the series only those blows that arise from the biomechanics of the movement. The blows should be easy to perform and have maximum force.

–   blows to different levels – alternate blows to the head and to the body between each other.

Combination

1. The opponent throws the jab.

2. The boxer slips to the left taking a step to the left or to the left-forward.

3. Next, the boxer performs the shuffle-twist to the left, throwing the left jab.

4. Immediately after landing the boxer delivers the rights cross to the opponent's head.

SECTION 9. THE SHUFFLE-TWIST TO THE LEFT

Combination

1. The opponent throws the jab.

2. The boxer slips to the left taking a step to the left-forward with the left foot.

3. Next, the boxer performs the shuffle-twist to the left, twisting clockwise.

4. Immediately after landing, the boxer delivers the punching series «the right uppercut to the head – the right uppercut to the head».

Combination

1. The boxer takes the falling step to the left-forward with the left foot, delivering the right punch to the opponent's head.

2. Next, the boxer performs the shuffle-twist to the left, twisting clockwise.

3. Immediately after landing, the boxer delivers the punching series «the right hook to the body – the right uppercut to the head».

SECTION 9. THE SHUFFLE-TWIST TO THE LEFT

Combination

1.   The boxer takes the falling step to the left-forward with the left foot, delivering the right punch to the opponent's head.

2.   Next, the boxer performs the shuffle-twist to the left, twisting clockwise.

3.   Immediately after landing, the boxer delivers the punching series «the right uppercut to the head – the left cross to the head».

Combination

1.   The boxer takes the falling step to the left-forward with the left foot, delivering the right punch to the opponent's body.

2. Next, the boxer performs the shuffle-twist to the left, throwing the left leaping hook.

3. Immediately after landing, the boxer delivers the punching series «the right uppercut to the head – the left cross to the head».

THE SHUFFLE-TWIST TO THE RIGHT

In this section, we consider such footwork technique as the «shuffle-twist to the right». The shuffle-twist to the right is a type of leap where a boxer pushes with the right foot and lands on the left foot, twisting counterclockwise and switching the stance to a southpaw. Simultaneously a boxer changes the angle of attack, moves to the right flank, and attacks from the new position. A boxer can perform this kind of leap from the basic stance, from a preliminary slip to the right, after a preliminary step to the right, or to the right-forward with the right foot. These positions create the biomechanical conditions for the «shuffle-twist to the right» leap.

BASIC TECHNIQUE

1. A boxer transfers body weight to the rear right leg. The right leg is charged and becomes a pushing one.

2. A boxer pushes off with his right foot, simultaneously undercutting his right foot from the left with his left foot.

3. A boxer jumps up, throws his right foot forward, simultaneously twisting his body counterclockwise to the left.

4. A boxer lands on his left foot. At the final position, the right foot is placed forward and the body weight is shifted to the left foot.

A slip to the right – a shuffle-twist to the right

To strengthen the leap, a boxer can previously transfer the body weight to the right leg slipping to the right. The right leg is charged and becomes the pushing leg. As a result, the leap is performed according to the scheme «a slip to the right – a shuffle-twist to the right».

If a boxer is at a long range, the leap «shuffle-twist to the left» can be performed with a preliminary step to the right or right-forward with the right foot.

The consistent technique for this footwork maneuver is as follows:

1. A boxer takes a step to the right-forward (or to the right) with the right foot and slips to the right, transferring body weight to the right leg.

2. A boxer pushes off with his right foot, simultaneously undercutting his right foot from the left with his left foot.

3. A boxer jumps up and forward, throws his right foot forward, simultaneously twisting his body counterclockwise to the left.

4. A boxer lands on his left foot. At the final position, the right foot is placed forward, and the body weight is shifted to the left foot.

SWITCHING THE STANCE AND ANGLE OF ATTACK

With the «shuffle-twist to the right» the boxer can switch his stance and change the angle of attack. By leaping, the boxer moves to the left relative to the opponent, approaches the opponent from the left flank, and switches from the orthodox stance to the southpaw stance. After landing, the right foot is in front, the body weight is on the left foot, and the body structure is charged to punch with the left hand.

The diagram of the leap is shown below. A boxer moves to the right and switches his stance from the orthodox to the southpaw. Most of the body weight is on the rear left leg after the leap.

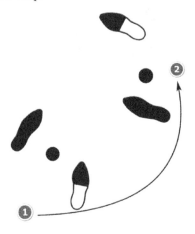

DEFENSE BY THE SHUFFLE-TWIST TO THE RIGHT

The technique can be used to defend against straight blows with both left and right hands.

1. The opponent throws a jab.

2. The boxer takes a step to the right-forward with his right foot, slipping to the right.

3. The boxer performs the «shuffle-twist to the right», twisting counterclockwise.

Defense against a left hook

This footwork tool can be combined with the bob and weave technique. In this case, the maneuver is performed according to the scheme «bob and weave to the right – shuffle-twist to the right».

1. The opponent delivers the left hook to the head.

2. The boxer bobs and weaves to the right, diving under the opponent's left hook.

3. The boxer transfers body weight to the right leg, pushes with the right foot and performs the «shuffle-twist to the right», twisting counterclockwise and going behind the opponent's back.

SECTION 10. THE SHUFFLE-TWIST TO THE RIGHT

Execution by Mike Tyson

In the photos below Kevin Rooney trains Mike Tyson. He delivers the left hook. Mike dives under the opponent's blow, stepping with his right foot to the right. The body weight is transferred to the right leg. The position is biomechanically comfortable for performing the «shuffle-twist to the right». Leaping, Mike twists his whole body counterclockwise and lands beyond the opponent's back.

ATTACKS BY THE SHUFFLE-TWIST TO THE RIGHT

PREPARATORY BLOWS BEFORE THE LEAP

Before the leap, a boxer may throw preliminary punches. Basically, these are the left-hand blows using the falling step with the right foot. These blows create the biomechanical conditions for the leap. Such blows fully load the right leg with the weight and the right foot becomes the pushing one. Therefore, these blows can be used as preparatory for the leap.

To strengthen this type of blows, it is advisable to slip preliminary to the left, charging the left leg for the subsequent push.

The photos below show possible preliminary blows using the falling step to the right-forward with the right foot before the shuffle-twist to the right – a left straight to the head, a left straight to the body, a left hook to the head.

SINGLE BLOWS WITH THE LEAP

Twisting clockwise, it is possible to throw leaping blows with the right hand. These leaping blows can be independent, then they are delivered in a forceful manner and are often knockout blows. They can also be part of more complex punching combinations, where the main punch is delivered after landing. In this case, leaping blows are delivered lightly and divert the attention of the opponent.

1. The boxer takes a step to the right-forward with his right foot (or to the right) and performs the «shuffle-twist to the right».

2. Leaping, the boxer delivers one of the possible leaping blows with the right hand – a right straight, a right hook or a right uppercut to the head.

BLOWS AFTER THE LEAP

In complex attacks using this footwork technique, the main punch in the series is the left hand punch after leaping and landing. When landing, the body weight is transferred to the left foot, so the entire body is charged with the left blow. The stance is strong and stable, the center of the body does not go beyond the support area. Therefore, the left punch will be heavy, powerful, and often a knockout blow. After leaping, the boxer can deliver a left cross, a left uppercut, a left hook to the head, a left hook to the body.

PUNCHING COMBINATIONS AFTER LANDING

Immediately after landing, the boxer can attack the opponent not only with a single blow but with one of the possible peekaboo punching combinations. Consider them in order.

The shuffle-twist to the right – the left uppercut to the head – the left uppercut to the head

1. The boxer performs the «shuffle-twist to the right», twisting counterclockwise.

2. Immediately after landing, the boxer delivers the punching series «the left uppercut to the head – the left uppercut to the head», keeping the weight on the left leg.

The shuffle-twist to the right – the left hook to the body – the left uppercut to the head

1.   The boxer performs the «shuffle-twist to the right», twisting counterclockwise.

2.   Immediately after landing, the boxer delivers the punching series «the left hook to the body – the left uppercut to the head», keeping the weight on the left leg.

The shuffle-twist to the right – the left uppercut to the head – the right cross to the head

1. The boxer performs the «shuffle-twist to the right», twisting counterclockwise.

2. Immediately after landing, the boxer delivers the punching series «the left uppercut to the head – the right cross to the head».

COMBINATORICS OF PUNCHING COMBINATIONS

So, when using the shuffle-twist to the right, blows can be delivered at any stage in combinational boxing peekaboo:

1. Blows before the shuffle-twist to the right (both single and series).

2. Blows with the shuffle-twist to the right with the right hand.

3. Blows after the shuffle-twist to the right (both singles and series).

The most complete punching combinations will be series using blows before the shuffle-twist to the right, blows with the shuffle-twist to the right, and blows after landing (in a total of 3 to 7 punches). The shortest punching combination will be a combination with a single blow after landing. The blows can be different and in different combinations. From this comes the punch combinatorics. Let's consider an example of building a multi-punch combination, using the shuffle-twist to the right.

1. The boxer takes the falling step to the right-forward with the right foot, delivering the left straight to the opponent's body.

2. The boxer pushes with the right foot and performs the «shuffle-twist to the right», simultaneously throwing the right leaping hook.

4.   Immediately after landing, the boxer delivers the punching series «the left hook to the body – the left uppercut to the head».

Similarly, it is possible to combine other punch combinations based on the leap « shuffle-twist to the right». The main requirements for composing a punching series are:

–   economy of motion – the punch series should not be overloaded with a large number of blows.

–   biomechanical basis for the blows – include in the series only those blows that arise from the biomechanics of the movement. The blows should be easy to perform and have maximum force.

–   blows to different levels – alternate blows to the head and to the body between each other.

SECTION 10. THE SHUFFLE-TWIST TO THE RIGHT

Combination

1. The opponent throws a jab to the head.

2. The boxer takes a step to the right-forward with his right foot, slipping to the right.

3. The boxer pushes with the right foot and performs the «shuffle-twist to the right», simultaneously throwing the leaping right jab to the opponent's head.

4. Immediately after landing, the boxer delivers the left cross to the opponent's head.

Combination

1.   The opponent throws a jab to the head.

2.   The boxer pushes with the right foot and performs the «shuffle-twist to the right», simultaneously throwing the right leaping hook to the opponent's head.

3.   Immediately after landing, the boxer delivers the left hook to the opponent's head.

SECTION 10. THE SHUFFLE-TWIST TO THE RIGHT

Combination

1. The opponent throws a jab to the head.

2. The boxer takes a step to the right-forward with his right foot, slipping to the right.

3. The boxer performs the «shuffle-twist to the right», twisting counterclockwise.

4. Immediately after landing, the boxer delivers the punching series «the left uppercut to the head – the left uppercut to the head», keeping the weight on the left leg.

Combination

1. The opponent throws a jab.

2. The boxer slips to the left.

3. The boxer takes the falling step to the right-forward with the right foot, delivering the left hook to the opponent's head.

4. The boxer performs the «shuffle-twist to the right», twisting counterclockwise.

5. Immediately after landing, the boxer delivers the left uppercut to the opponent's head.

SECTION 10. THE SHUFFLE-TWIST TO THE RIGHT

Combination

1. The opponent delivers the left hook to the head.

2. The boxer bobs and weaves to the right, diving under the opponent's left hook and transferring body weight to the right leg.

3. The boxer pushes with the right foot and performs the «shuffle-twist to the right», simultaneously throwing the right leaping hook.

4. Immediately after landing, the boxer delivers the left hook to the opponent's head.

Combination

1. The boxer takes the falling step to the right-forward with the right foot, delivering the left straight to the opponent's body.

2. The boxer pushes with the right foot and performs the «shuffle-twist to the right», simultaneously throwing the right leaping hook.

3. Immediately after landing, the boxer delivers the punching series «the left uppercut to the head – the right cross to the head».

SECTION 10. THE SHUFFLE-TWIST TO THE RIGHT

Combination

1. The boxer performs the «shuffle-twist to the right», twisting counterclockwise.

2. Immediately after landing, the boxer delivers the punching series «the left hook to the body – the left uppercut to the head», keeping the weight on the left leg.

THE FALLING JUMP TO THE LEFT-FORWARD

The next variant of changing the angle of attack is the falling jump to the left-forward. This type of boxing maneuver resembles jumping across a puddle when a person pushes with one foot and lands on the other foot. The difference is that a boxer does not jump straight forward, but diagonally to the left-forward. Some analysts call this type of jump a sliding leap. This emphasizes that a boxer does not jump up, but drops his weight as if sliding during the jump. We suggest another name – the falling jump because this footwork technique resembles a falling step. The difference is that a boxer lengthens the falling step by jumping.

The falling jump to the left-forward is a type of jump where a boxer pushes with the right foot and lands on the left foot, moving diagonally to the left flank relative to an opponent and switching the stance to a southpaw.

BASIC TECHNIQUE

1. A boxer pushes with his right foot. Simultaneously his left foot takes the falling jump to the left-forward.

2. The right pushing foot follows the left foot after pushing.

3. During the jump the body slips to the left and the body weight drops down.

4. A boxer lands on the left foot and the right foot pulls to the left foot.

5. The head turns to the right and looks at an opponent.

The falling jump to the left-forward with a preliminary slip to the right

To strengthen the falling jump to the left-forward, a boxer can shift body weight to the right leg preliminarily. By slipping to the right, the right leg is charged and becomes the pushing leg. As a result, the jump is performed according to the scheme «slip to the right – jump to the left».

A boxer can also slip to the right by stepping to the right (or right-forward) with the right foot. It speeds up the body mass preliminarily, and then the falling jump to the left-forward will be easier and more amplified.

SWITCHING THE STANCE AND ANGLE OF ATTACK

With this maneuver, the boxer gets closer to the opponent, moves to the left forward, changes the angle of attack, and approaches the opponent from the left flank. This footwork technique changes the stance. The boxer switches from the orthodox stance to the southpaw stance by jumping. After landing, the right foot is in front, the body weight is on the left foot, and the body structure is charged to punch with the left hand.

The diagram of the jump is shown below. Boxer moves to the left and switches his stance from the orthodox to the southpaw. Most of the body weight is on the rear left leg after the jump.

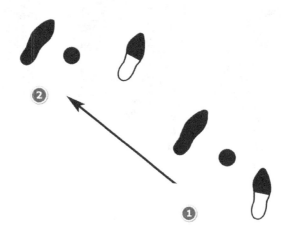

SECTION 11. THE FALLING JUMP TO THE LEFT-FORWARD

Execution by Mike Tyson

Below, Michael Tyson is at close range and performs this type of footwork after slipping to the right. As you can see, Tyson is not just taking a wide step, but he is doing a wide jump with the left foot. By jumping Tyson occupies a southpaw stance.

ENTERING CLOSE FIGHTING BY THE FALLING JUMP TO THE LEFT-FORWARD

This footwork technique can be used to close to the opponent from a long distance, change the angle of attack and attack the opponent from the left flank.

1. The boxer steps forward with his right foot, slipping to the right.

2. Immediately after slipping, the boxer takes the falling jump to the left-forward, pushing with the right foot and landing on the left foot.

Feature. This footwork trick sharply shortens the distance and allows a boxer to break into close range by changing the stance and angle of attack.

SECTION 11. THE FALLING JUMP TO THE LEFT-FORWARD

DEFENSE BY THE FALLING JUMP TO THE LEFT-FORWARD

The footwork technique can be used both without punches and with punches. If the technique is used without punches, it will be a defensive option against the opponent's straight blows with both left and right hands.

Defense against a jab

1. The opponent throws a jab to the head.

2. The boxer takes the falling jump to the left, pushing with the right foot and landing on the left foot.

Defense against a right straight

1. The opponent throws the right straight punch to the head.

2. The boxer takes the falling jump to the left, pushing with the right foot and landing on the left foot.

Execution by Mike Tyson

In the photos below, the opponent delivers the right straight punch. Tyson pushes with his right foot, slips to his left, and jumps to the left-forward, landing on the left foot. As a result, he moves to the left flank, cutting the angle.

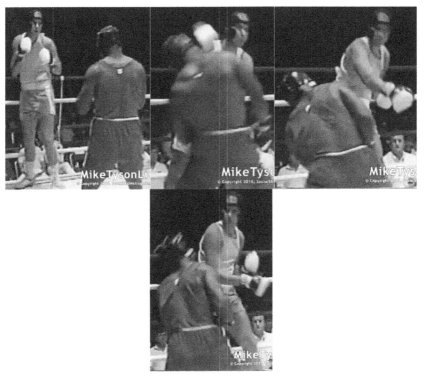

Defense against a right straight (the second variant)

1. The opponent throws the right straight punch to the head.

2. The boxer steps forward with his right foot, slipping to the right.

3. The boxer takes the falling jump to the left-forward, pushing with the right foot and landing on the left foot.

ATTACKS BY THE FALLING JUMP TO THE LEFT-FORWARD

PREPARATORY BLOWS BEFORE THE JUMP

The falling jump to the left-forward may be preceded by blows. These are the left-hand blows, transferring body weight to the right leg, as well as blows with the left hand using the falling step to the right-forward with the right foot. Such blows create the biomechanical conditions for the jump.

This type of blow creates a critical point of equilibrium in the body. The body weight is transferred to the right leg after a blow and the body mass at this point tends to fall to the left under the action of gravity. The projection of the center of the body goes beyond the support area.

As a result, on one side the right leg is charged for the push, and on the other side the body mass tends to fall to the left. The boxer uses this distribution of biomechanical forces to jump to the left-forward. The jump is performed much faster, more abruptly, and with less physical effort. Therefore, such blows can be used as preparatory blows for the falling jump to the left-forward.

Let's consider the technique of preliminary blows in more detail.

1.   The boxer steps forward with his left foot, slipping to the left.

2.   The boxer lands a left uppercut using the falling step to the right-forward with his right foot. Body weight is shifted to the right leg.

3.   Immediately after blowing, the boxer jumps to the left-forward with his left foot, pushing with the right foot and landing on the left foot.

In addition to the uppercut, a similar distribution of biomechanical forces can be created by a left hook to the body and a left hook to the head. Next, the boxer performs the falling to the left-forward, moving to the left flank and changing the angle of attack. After landing, the boxer can deliver one of the possible punching combinations (discussed below).

SINGLE BLOWS WITH THE FALLING JUMP

Jumping to the left-forward, a boxer can throw a blow. A blow is not a knockout one, but it allows a boxer to hide the beginning of the jump and distract an opponent's attention. An opponent may be frightened by a blow, covers himself with gloves and so for a moment the boxer is out of sight. Such a blow with the falling jump to the left-forward is an active method of defense because there is less chance that an opponent will be able to blow.

The jab with the falling jump to the left-forward

1. The boxer pushes with the right foot and jumps to the left-forward.

2. Jumping, the boxer throws the left jab to the opponent's head.

Feature. The blow is very sharp and fast as it is applied with the falling jump. It is necessary to throw and sharply draw the left hand towards yourself.

The right straight with the falling jump to the left-forward

1. The boxer pushes with the right foot and jumps to the left-forward.

2. Jumping, the boxer throws the right straight to the opponent's head.

Feature. The blow is very sharp and fast because it is applied with the falling jump. It is necessary to throw and sharply draw the right hand towards yourself.

BLOWS AFTER THE FALLING JUMP

The falling jump to the left-forward can be used to attack. The jump allows a boxer to move to the left flank, switch the stance to the southpaw and change the angle of attack. This is unexpected for the opponent, so the footwork trick can lead to a successful attack. In most cases, the main blow is the one after landing. After landing, the body weight is transferred to the left leg. The leg and torso are charged with the left hand punch. Therefore, the punch is heavy and often a knockout punch. The photos below show how the boxer delivers a left hook or left cross after the falling jump to the left-forward.

Basic technique

1. The boxer performs the falling jump to the left-forward, pushing with the right foot and landing on the left foot.

2. Immediately after landing, a boxer delivers a left cross or a left hook to the head.

Execution by Mike Tyson

Below is the combination described above, performed by Michael Tyson. Tyson takes the falling jump to the left-forward. After landing on his left foot, Tyson is loaded with the left hand and delivers a left hook.

PUNCHING COMBINATIONS AFTER LANDING

After the falling jump to the left-forward and delivering the main punch with the left hand, the boxer can continue with one of the punching combinations, characteristic of peekaboo. Consider them in order.

The falling jump to the left-forward – the left cross – the right uppercut to the head – the right uppercut to the head

1. The boxer performs the falling jump to the left-forward.

2. Immediately after landing, the boxer delivers the left cross or the left hook to the head.

3. Then the boxer delivers the punching series «the right uppercut to the head – the right uppercut to the head».

The falling jump to the left-forward – the left cross – the right hook to the body – the right uppercut to the head

1. The boxer performs the falling jump to the left-forward.

2. Immediately after landing, the boxer delivers the left cross or the left hook to the head.

3. Then the boxer delivers the punching series «the right hook to the body – the right uppercut to the head».

SECTION 11. THE FALLING JUMP TO THE LEFT-FORWARD

The falling jump to the left-forward – the left cross – the right uppercut to the head – the left cross to the head

1. The boxer performs the falling jump to the left-forward.

2. Immediately after landing, the boxer delivers the left cross or the left hook to the head.

3. Then the boxer delivers the punching series «the right uppercut to the head – the left cross to the head».

COMBINATORICS OF PUNCHING COMBINATIONS

So, when using the falling jump to the left-forward blows can be delivered at any stage in combinational boxing peekaboo:

1. Blows before the falling jump to the left-forward (both single and series).
2. Blows with the falling jump to the left-forward (both left and right hand).
3. Blows after the falling jump to the left-forward (both singles and series).

The most complete punching combinations will be series using blows before the falling jump to the left-forward, blows with the falling jump, and blows after landing (in a total of 3 to 7 punches). The shortest punching combination will be a combination with a single blow after landing. The blows can be different and in different combinations. From this comes the punch combinatorics. Let's consider an example of building a multi-punch combination, using the falling jump to the left-forward.

1. The boxer delivers a series «jab – right cross to the head» and adds the right hook to the body, taking the falling step to the right-forward with the right foot.

SECTION 11. THE FALLING JUMP TO THE LEFT-FORWARD

1. The boxer performs the falling jump to the left-forward, throwing the right straight at the same time.

2. Immediately after landing, the boxer delivers a left cross or a left hook to the head.

3. Next, the boxer delivers a series of punches «right hook to the body – right uppercut to the head».

Combination

1. The boxer performs the falling jump to the left-forward, throwing the jab at the same time.

2. Immediately after landing, the boxer delivers the left hook to the opponent's head.

SECTION 11. THE FALLING JUMP TO THE LEFT-FORWARD

Execution by Mike Tyson

Below is the combination described above and performed by Mike Tyson. Tyson takes the falling jump to the left-forward, throwing the jab at the same time. Landing on his left foot, Tyson switches to the southpaw stance and charges the body for a left-handed punch. From the occupied position, the boxer delivers the left hook to the opponent's head.

Combination

1. The boxer performs the falling jump to the left-forward, throwing the jab at the same time.

2. Immediately after landing, the boxer delivers the left cross to the opponent's head.

SECTION 11. THE FALLING JUMP TO THE LEFT-FORWARD

Combination

1. The boxer slips to the left and from this position throws a series of blows: «left hook – right hook – left hook».

2. After the last left hook, the boxer performs the falling jump to the left-forward.

3. Immediately after landing, the boxer delivers the left hook to the opponent's head.

Execution by Mike Tyson

Below Michael Tyson performs the combination described above. Tyson slips to the left, and then delivers the punching combination «left hook – right hook – left hook». The body weight is shifted to the right leg after the last blow.

To move to the left flank, Tyson uses the falling jump to the left-forward. Landing on his left foot, Tyson switches to the southpaw stance and charges the body for a left-handed punch. From the occupied position, the boxer delivers the left hook to the opponent's head.

Combination

1. The boxer takes the falling step to the left-forward with the left foot and delivers the right punch and then the left uppercut to the opponent's head, transferring body weight to the right leg.

2. The boxer performs the falling jump to the left-forward.

3. Immediately after landing, the boxer delivers the left cross to the opponent's head.

Execution by Mike Tyson

Below Michael Tyson performs the combination described above.

Tyson takes the falling step with his left foot and lands the right cross to the head. Next, Tyson immediately lands the left uppercut to the head. The body weight is shifted to the right leg. To move to the left flank, Tyson uses the falling jump to the left-forward. Landing on his left foot, Tyson switches to the southpaw stance and charges the body for a left-handed punch. From the occupied position, the boxer delivers the left cross to the opponent's head.

Combination

1. The boxer takes a step with the left foot forward delivering the left straight to the opponent's body.

2. The boxer performs the falling jump to the left-forward.

3. Immediately after landing, the boxer delivers the left hook to the opponent's head.

Execution by Mike Tyson

Below Michael Tyson performs the combination described above.

Tyson attacks with a jab to the opponent's body.

Then Tyson pushes with his right foot and takes the falling jump to the left-forward, cutting an angle.

After landing Mike attacks from the left side with the left hook to the opponent's head.

THE FALLING JUMP TO THE RIGHT-FORWARD

The next footwork technique for cutting angles is the falling jump to the right-forward. This is a similar and symmetrical technique to the falling jump to left-forward. The falling jump to the right-forward is a type of jump where a boxer pushes with the left foot and lands on the right foot, moving diagonally to the right flank relative to an opponent.

Previously, the body weight is transferred to the left leg. The left leg is charged and becomes a push. This can be done from a basic stance, from a bob, or from a slip to the left. From these positions, it is convenient to jump to the right-forward.

BASIC TECHNIQUE

1. A boxer pushes with his left foot. Simultaneously, his right foot takes the falling jump to the right-forward.

2. The left pushing foot follows the right foot after pushing.

3. During the jump the body slips to the right and the body weight drops down.

4. A boxer lands on the right foot, the left foot pulls to the right foot.

5. The head turns to the left and looks at an opponent.

The falling jump to the right-forward with a preliminary slip to the left

To strengthen the falling jump to the right-forward, a boxer can shift body weight to the left leg preliminarily. By slipping to the left, the left leg is charged and becomes the pushing leg. As a result, the jump is performed according to the scheme «slip to the left – jump to the right».

A boxer can also slip to the left by stepping with the left foot. Step forward speeds up the body mass preliminarily, and then the falling jump to the right-forward will be easier and more amplified.

SWITCHING THE STANCE AND ANGLE OF ATTACK

Using this footwork maneuver, the boxer gets closer to the opponent, moves to the right-forward, changes the angle of attack, and approaches the opponent from the right flank. There is no switch of a stance in this jump. The boxer stays in the orthodox stance after landing, but sharply changes his position relative to his opponent. After landing, the left foot is in front, the body weight is on the right foot, and the body structure is charged to punch with the right hand.

The diagram of the jump is shown below. Boxer moves to the right and changes the angle of attack. The stance stays an orthodox one. Most of the body weight is on the rear right leg after the jump.

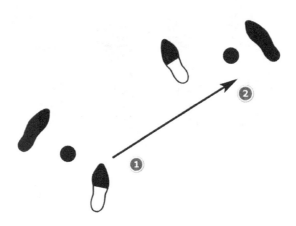

SECTION 12. THE FALLING JUMP TO THE RIGHT-FORWARD

Execution by Kevin Rooney

Standing in the frontal stance, Kevin Rooney pushes with his left foot and takes the falling jump to the right-forward with his right foot, landing on his right foot.

ENTERING CLOSE FIGHTING BY THE FALLING JUMP TO THE RIGHT-FORWARD

This footwork technique can be used to close to the opponent from a long distance, change the angle of attack and attack the opponent from the right flank.

1. The boxer steps forward with his right foot and then steps forward with his left foot, slipping to the left.

2. Immediately after slipping, the boxer takes the falling jump to the right-forward.

Execution by Mike Tyson

Being at a long distance Tyson gets close to his opponent with normal steps, taking a step forward with the right foot. Tyson then takes a step forward with his left foot and imitates a slip to the left, deceiving his opponent.

After shifting his body weight to his left foot, Tyson sharply pushes with his left foot and jumps to the right-forward with his right foot, landing on his right foot.

DEFENSE BY THE FALLING JUMP TO THE RIGHT-FORWARD

This footwork technique can be used as a defensive maneuver against the straight blows of an opponent.

Defense against a right straight

1. The opponent delivers the right straight punch to the head.

2. The boxer sharply takes the falling jump to the right-forward, pushing off with his left foot.

Defense against a jab

1. The opponent throws a jab to the head.

2. The boxer steps forward with his left foot, slipping to the left.

3. The boxer sharply takes the falling jump to the right-forward, pushing off with his left foot.

ATTACKS BY THE FALLING JUMP TO THE RIGHT-FORWARD

PREPARATORY BLOWS BEFORE THE JUMP

The falling jump to the right-forward may be preceded by blows. These blows create the biomechanical conditions for the jump. These are blows with the right hand, partly transferring body weight to the left leg. This type of blow creates a critical point of equilibrium in the body. The body weight is transferred to the left leg after a blow and the body mass at this point tends to fall to the right under the action of gravity. The projection of the center of the body goes beyond the support area.

As a result, on one side the left leg is charged for the push, and on the other side the body mass tends to fall to the right. The boxer uses this distribution of biomechanical forces to jump to the right-forward. The jump is performed much faster, more abruptly, and with less physical effort. Therefore, such blows can be used as preparatory blows for the falling jump to the right-forward.

SECTION 12. THE FALLING JUMP TO THE RIGHT-FORWARD

Let's consider the technique of the falling jump to the right-forward with a preliminary blow in more detail.

1.   The boxer lands a right uppercut using the falling step with the left foot to the left-forward. Body weight is shifted to the left leg.

2.   Immediately after blowing, the boxer jumps to the right-forward with his right foot, pushing with his left foot.

Execution by Mike Tyson

Tyson lands a right uppercut. The body weight is shifted to the left leg, and the body tilts to the right. There is a point of critical balance where the force of gravity causes the fall. Using the force of the fall, from this position, the boxer takes the falling jump to the right-forward – pushing with the left foot and making a wide step with the right foot to the right-forward.

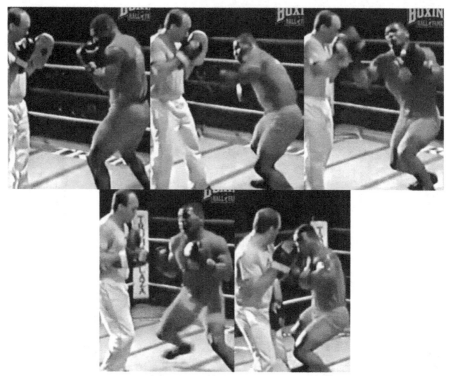

SECTION 12. THE FALLING JUMP TO THE RIGHT-FORWARD

Besides a right uppercut, a similar distribution of biomechanical forces can be created by a right hook to the body and a right straight to the head. Next, the boxer performs the falling jump to the right-forward, moving to the right flank and changing the angle of attack. After landing, the boxer can deliver one of the possible punching combinations (discussed below).

The falling jump to the right-forward may be preceded by another type of blows, which also creates the biomechanical conditions for the jump. These are blows with the right hand with fully transferring the body weight to the left leg. In this type of blows, the left leg is fully loaded with the weight of the boxer and becomes the pushing leg. A strong push with the left foot allows a boxer to jump to the right-forward.

If in the previous type of preliminary blows, the jump is performed more by gravity and fall, in this type of blows the jump is performed more by pushing with the left foot and muscular force. Therefore, these blows can be used as preparatory for the jump.

SECTION 12. THE FALLING JUMP TO THE RIGHT-FORWARD

The general scheme of such combinations is presented in the photos below:

1. The boxer delivers a right straight or right hook to the opponent's head, transferring his body weight to his left leg.

2. The boxer pushes off with his left foot and performs the falling jump to the right-forward, landing on the right foot.

SINGLE BLOWS WITH THE FALLING JUMP

Taking the falling jump to the right-forward, a boxer can throw a blow. The blow is not a knockout one, but it allows to hide the beginning of the jump and distract the opponent's attention. In addition, the blow can make an opponent to close in the shell. Thus, the boxer drops out of sight for a moment. Therefore, it is less likely that the opponent can strike, and the boxer has a better chance to successfully change the angle of attack.

The jab with the falling jump to the right-forward

1.   The boxer pushes with the left foot and jumps to the right-forward with the right foot, landing on the right foot.

2.   Jumping, the boxer throws the left jab to the opponent's head.

Feature. The jab is very sharp and fast as it is applied at the falling jump. It is necessary to throw and sharply draw the left hand towards yourself.

Execution by Mike Tyson

Tyson throws a jab with the falling jump to the right-forward. To do this, he pushes with his left foot and takes a wide jump to the right-forward with his right foot. When landing, his body weight is on his right foot, his body leans to the right and his head turns to the left.

The right straight with the falling jump to the right-forward

1.   The boxer pushes with the left foot and jumps to the right-forward with the right foot, landing on the right foot.

2.   Jumping, the boxer throws the right straight to the opponent's head.

Feature. The right straight is very sharp and fast as it is applied at the falling jump. It is necessary to throw and sharply draw the right hand towards yourself.

BLOWS AFTER THE FALLING JUMP

The falling jump to the right-forward can be used to attack. The jump allows a boxer to move to the left flank, switch the stance to the southpaw and change the angle of attack. This is unexpected for the opponent, so the footwork trick can lead to a successful attack. In most cases, the main blow is the one after landing. After landing, the body weight is transferred to the left leg. The leg and torso are charged with the left-hand blow. Therefore, the punch is heavy and often a knockout punch. The photos below show how the boxer delivers a left hook or left cross after the falling jump to the right-forward.

1. From the boxing stance, the boxer performs the falling jump to the right-forward.

2. Immediately after landing, the boxer delivers the right cross or right hook to the opponent's head.

Execution by Mike Tyson

From the fighting stance, Tyson uses the falling jump to the right-forward to attack the opponent from the right flank. He pushes with his left foot and takes the jump to the right-forward with his right foot, landing on his right foot. Tyson is now positioned at an angle to the opponent. From this position, Tyson delivers the heavy right cross, transferring the body weight to his left leg.

SECTION 12. THE FALLING JUMP TO THE RIGHT-FORWARD

PUNCHING COMBINATIONS AFTER LANDING

After the falling jump to the right-forward and delivering the main punch with the right hand, the boxer can continue with one of the punching combinations, characteristic of peekaboo. Consider them in order.

The falling jump to the right-forward – the right cross – the left uppercut to the head – the left uppercut to the head

1.   From the boxing stance, the boxer performs the falling jump to the right-forward.

2.   Immediately after landing, the boxer delivers the right cross or the right hook to the head.

3.   Then the boxer delivers the punching series «the left uppercut to the head – the left uppercut to the head».

The falling jump to the right-forward – the right cross – the left hook to the body – the left uppercut to the head

1. From the boxing stance, the boxer performs the falling jump to the right-forward.

2. Immediately after landing, the boxer delivers the right cross or the right hook to the head.

3. Then the boxer delivers the punching series «the left hook to the body – the left uppercut to the head».

SECTION 12. THE FALLING JUMP TO THE RIGHT-FORWARD

The falling jump to the right-forward – the right cross – the left uppercut to the head – the right cross to the head

1.   From the boxing stance, the boxer performs the falling jump to the right-forward.

2.   Immediately after landing, the boxer delivers the right cross or the right hook to the head.

3.   Then the boxer delivers a punching series «the left uppercut to the head – the right cross to the head».

COMBINATORICS OF PUNCHING COMBINATIONS

So, when using the falling jump to the right-forward, blows can be delivered at any stage in combinational boxing peekaboo:

1. Blows before the falling jump to the right-forward (both single and series).
2. Blows with the falling jump to the right-forward (both left and right hand).
3. Blows after the falling jump to the right-forward (both singles and series).

The most complete punching combinations will be series using blows before the falling jump to the left-forward, blows with the falling jump, and blows after landing (in a total of 3 to 7 punches). The shortest punching combination will be a combination with a single blow after landing. The blows can be different and in different combinations. From this comes the punch combinatorics. Let's consider an example of building a multi-punch combination, using the falling jump to the right-forward.

1. The boxer delivers a two-punch series «jab – right uppercut to the head».

2. From the boxing stance, the boxer performs the falling jump to the right-forward.

3. Immediately after landing, the boxer delivers the right cross or right hook to the head.

4. Then, the boxer delivers the punching series «left hook to the body – left uppercut to the head».

Combination

1. The boxer takes a step forward with his left foot, imitating a slip to the left, thus deceiving the opponent and provoking him to throw a jab.

2. The opponent throws a jab.

3. The boxer takes the falling jump to the right-forward, avoiding the opponent's jab.

4. Immediately after landing, the boxer delivers the cross to the head.

SECTION 12. THE FALLING JUMP TO THE RIGHT-FORWARD

Execution by Mike Tyson

Being at a long distance Tyson gets close to his opponent with normal steps, taking a step forward with the right foot. Tyson then takes a step forward with his left foot and imitates the slip to the left, deceiving his opponent and provoking him to throw a jab.

After shifting his body weight to his left foot, Tyson sharply pushes with his left foot and jumps to the right-forward with his right foot, landing on his right foot.

After landing on his right foot, Tyson immediately throws a right cross to the opponent's head.

Combination

1.   The boxer pushes with the left foot and jumps to the right-forward with the right foot.

2.   Jumping to the right-forward, the boxer throws the jab to the opponent's head.

3.   Immediately after landing, the boxer delivers the right cross to the opponent's head.

Execution by Mike Tyson

The photos below show Tyson's combination on boxing mitts. Tyson throws a jab, jumping to the right-forward. He pushes with his left foot, jumping to the right-forward with his right foot.

When landing, the body weight is on the right leg, the head turns to the left. From this position, the boxer delivers the heavy right cross to the opponent's head.

Combination

1. The boxer delivers a series of blows «left jab – right cross to the head».

2. The boxer pushes with the left foot, performing the falling jump to the right-forward.

3. Immediately after landing, the boxer delivers the right cross to the opponent's head.

SECTION 12. THE FALLING JUMP TO THE RIGHT-FORWARD

Execution by Mike Tyson

Here Tyson attacks the opponent with a right cross to the head. His opponent covers up. Next, Tyson loses his balance to the right, pushes with his left foot, and takes a jump to the right-forward with his right foot. Thereby, Tyson moves to the right flank of the attack and gets in the perfect position for the strong right cross to the opponent's head.

Combination

1. The boxer delivers the right straight to the opponent's head and immediately slips to the right, stepping to the right with the right foot.

2. From the right slipping position, the boxer delivers the right uppercut to the opponent's head.

3. The boxer pushes with the left foot and jumps to the right-forward.

4. Immediately after landing, the boxer delivers the right cross to the head.

SECTION 12. THE FALLING JUMP TO THE RIGHT-FORWARD

Execution by Mike Tyson

Tyson lands the right straight using the falling step with the left foot. Next, the boxer takes a step to the right with his right foot (the shift to the right) and slips to the right, transferring his body weight to his right foot.

From this position, the boxer delivers the right uppercut to the opponent's head. The body weight is shifted to the left leg again. Next, Michael pushes off with his left foot and takes the falling jump to the right-forward with his right foot.

Immediately after landing on the right foot, the boxer delivers the heavy right cross to the opponent's head, transferring his body weight to his left leg.

231

Combination

1. The boxer throws the jab to the opponent's body, ducking to the right and stepping forward with his left foot.

2. From this position, the boxer delivers the right uppercut to the opponent's head.

3. The boxer pushes with the left foot and jumps to the right-forward with the right foot.

4. Immediately after landing, the boxer delivers the right cross to the opponent's head.

Execution by Mike Tyson

Tyson steps forward with his left foot and throws the left straight to the opponent's body, ducking to the right.

Next, the boxer lands the right uppercut to the opponent's head.

Immediately after the uppercut, the boxer takes the falling jump to the right-forward – pushing with his left foot and taking a wide step to the right-forward with his right foot. After landing, the boxer delivers the right cross to the opponent's head.

233

Combination

1. The boxer throws the jab to the opponent's head stepping to the left-forward with his left foot and slipping to the left.

2. From this position, the boxer delivers the right uppercut to the opponent's head.

3. The boxer pushes with the left foot and jumps to the right-forward with his right foot.

4. Immediately after landing, the boxer delivers the right cross to the opponent's head.

SECTION 12. THE FALLING JUMP TO THE RIGHT-FORWARD

Execution by Mike Tyson

Tyson throws the left jab to the opponent's head using the falling step with the left foot to the left-forward falling step to the left-forward with the left foot, slipping to the left. From this position, the boxer delivers the left uppercut and adds the right cross to the opponent's head.

The body weight is shifted to the left leg. Next, Mike takes the falling jump to the right-forward, pushing with his left foot. Immediately after landing, the boxer delivers the right cross to the opponent's head.

COMBINATIONS OF JUMPS

Jump and leap combinations play a special role in peekaboo. The alternation of different methods of footwork is the basis of complex punch combinations and complex variants of defense.

The combination of jumps depends primarily on the distance to an opponent. The most variations are possible if an opponent is at a long distance. In this case, the peekaboo boxer uses one footwork trick to get closer, and the second one to change his stance and angle of attack. In close combat, combinations of jumps are limited because the boxer is close to an opponent and one footwork trick is enough to change the angle of attack and stance.

Tactical scheme of jumps

Boxing is a constant dynamic. Footwork maneuvers are used to chase an opponent, often one following the other, in various combinations. Therefore, it is important to know not only the technique of individual jumps but also the tactical scheme of the footwork. The tactical scheme of the footwork is a sequence of possible jumps from the biomechanics point of view. The skill to combine different footwork tricks is an advantage in dynamics and the ability to quickly change the position relative to an opponent, creating unexpected angles of attack.

The reference point in tactical analysis

The basic technique of footwork is the shuffle forward. It is this leap that is most often used to attack from a long distance, to get close to the opponent, to press, and to pursue the opponent. All other jumps and leaps are combined with this method of footwork. Therefore, consider possible combinations where the first leap is a shuffle forward.

Shuffle forward – shuffle-twist to the right

1. A boxer performs the shuffle forward.

2. From inertia, a boxer takes a step to the right with his right foot, slipping to the right (the shift to the right). Body weight is shifted to the right leg.

3. A boxer performs the shuffle-twist counterclockwise.

1. A boxer performs the shuffle forward.

2. While landing, a boxer slips to the right. The body weight is transferred to the right leg.

3. A boxer performs the shuffle-twist counterclockwise.

Shuffle forward – shuffle-twist to the left

1. A boxer performs the shuffle forward.

2. While landing, a boxer slips to the left. The body weight is transferred to the left leg.

3. A boxer performs the shuffle-twist clockwise.

Shuffle forward – shuffle to the right

1. A boxer performs the shuffle forward.

2. From inertia, a boxer takes a step to the right with his right foot, slipping to the right (the shift to the right). Body weight is shifted to the right leg.

3. A boxer performs the shuffle to the right.

1. A boxer performs the shuffle forward.

2. While landing, a boxer slips to the right. The body weight is transferred to the right leg.

3. A boxer performs the shuffle to the right.

Shuffle forward – shuffle to the left

1. A boxer performs the shuffle forward.

2. While landing, a boxer slips to the left. The body weight is transferred to the left leg.

3. A boxer performs the shuffle to the left.

Combination

Below is a simulation of one of Tyson's knockouts in a counterattacking version. The boxer steps forward with his left foot and throws the leaping jab, simultaneously with the opponent's jab, taking the shuffle forward. After landing, the boxer delivers the right cross. Then the boxer performs the shuffle to the left and after landing, the boxer delivers the right hook.

Execution by Mike Tyson

Tyson steps forward with his left foot from a long range, transfers body weight to it and performs the shuffle forward, throwing the leaping counter jab under the opponent's jab. After landing, the body weight is on the right leg.

From this position, Tyson lands the right cross, transferring body weight to his left leg and slipping to the left.

Then, Tyson executes «the shuffle to the left», switching the stance. Tyson does not deliver the right blow, as the opponent is knocked out by the previous right cross.

Shuffle forward – falling jump to the left

1. A boxer performs the shuffle forward.

2. Immediately after landing on his right foot, a boxer pushes with his right foot and makes a jump with his left foot to the left-forward, performing the falling jump to the left-forward.

Execution by Mike Tyson

The boxer pursues his opponent taking two consecutive footwork tricks – the shuffle forward and the falling jump to the left. The jumps are made one after the other, together, without pauses – the shuffle forward turns into the explosive falling jump to the left-forward.

Combination

1.   The boxer performs the shuffle forward, ducking to the right and throwing the jab to the opponent's body.

2.   Immediately after landing, the boxer performs the falling jump to the left-forward.

3.   Immediately after landing, the boxer delivers the left cross to the head.

Execution by Mike Tyson

Tyson performs the shuffle forward, ducking to the right and throwing the jab to the opponent's body. Immediately after landing on his right foot, Tyson pushes with his right foot and makes a jump with his left foot to the left-forward, performing the falling jump to the left-forward. Immediately after landing, the boxer delivers the left cross to the head.

Shuffle forward – falling jump to the right

1. A boxer performs the shuffle forward.

2. While landing, a boxer slips to the left.

3. A boxer performs the falling jump to the right-forward, pushing off with the left foot and jumping to the right-forward with the right foot.

The combination «shuffle forward – falling jump to the right» may be performed without a binding slip to the left. In this case, a boxer after the shuffle forward by inertia transfers the body weight on the left leg without slipping to the left and then pushes with the left foot, making a broad jump to the right-forward with the right foot. This variation of the combination can be applied if there is no threat of a counterattack blow.

Execution by Mike Tyson

Tyson takes a step forward with the left foot and performs the shuffle forward, throwing the jab. After landing Tyson performs the falling jump to the right. The jumps are made one after the other, without pauses – the shuffle forward turns into the explosive falling jump to the right.

SECTION 13. COMBINATIONS OF JUMPS

The first footwork technique in the combination can be not only the shuffle forward but also the falling jump to the left-forward or the right-forward. Consider the possible combinations of this type.

Falling jump to the left-forward – shuffle-twist to the left

1. A boxer performs the falling jump to the left-forward, pushing off with the right foot and jumping to the left-forward with the left foot.

2. While landing, a boxer transfers the body weight to the left leg.

3. Immediately after landing, a boxer performs the shuffle-twist clockwise, pushing with the left foot.

Execution by Mike Tyson

Tyson slips to the right, body weight is shifted to the right leg. The right leg becomes the pushing leg. Tyson performs the falling step to the right-forward, pushing with the right foot and simultaneously jumping to the left-forward with the left foot. While landing, the boxer transfers the body weight to the left leg.

Immediately after landing, the boxer performs the shuffle-twist clockwise and slips to the right when landing.

This footwork combination technique allowed Tyson to get close to his opponent and enter from long range to close range at a new angle.

Falling jump to the right-forward – shuffle-twist to the right

1. A boxer performs the falling jump to the right-forward, pushing off with the left foot and jumping to the right-forward with the right foot.

2. While landing, a boxer transfers the body weight to the right leg.

3. Immediately after landing, a boxer performs the shuffle-twist counterclockwise.

Execution by Mike Tyson

The opponent lands a jab. Tyson takes a step to the left with the left foot, threatening to attack. The opponent groups himself to defend and covers up. Tyson performs the falling jump to the right-forward. Immediately after landing, the boxer makes the shuffle-twist counterclockwise.

FOOTWORK TRAINING

In fact, it's very simple: to learn how to box, a boxer has to master the footwork. Constantly practicing footwork skills is a necessary part of boxing training. Boxing footwork is the most important skill for any boxer, so take the time to practice and improve your mobility. By practicing footwork drills, a boxer will give real dynamism to attacking boxing style.

To practice footwork, Tyson and Rooney used one simple exercise, but on closer analysis, it is very complex and allows practicing essentially all kinds of tricks. The essence of this drill is that the boxer performs different types of jumps in front of his partner. Instead of a partner, a boxer can use a punching bag or marks on the floor.

Training exercises consist of a set of different jumps in a certain sequence. The boxer repeats a set of all jumps.

Such exercises are very good for training footwork, strengthening the muscles and tendons of the legs, increasing coordination, jumping ability, and speed. All this has an effect in the fight and improves the footwork.

Before proceeding to a set of jumps, it is important to work out the biomechanics of each jump separately. Training combinations of jumps can be complicated in various ways by adding new jumps or, on the contrary, by simplifying. Let's consider one of the possible training combinations of jumps.

Training combination

1.   The boxer is in a frontal stance in front of his partner.

2.   The boxer pushes off, jumping up and twisting clockwise 180 degrees so that he lands with his back to his partner.

3.   Immediately after landing, the boxer makes a reverse jump counterclockwise, to return to a frontal stance facing his partner.

4. The boxer pushes off with the left foot and jumps to the right-forward with the right foot, performing the falling jump to the right-forward.

5. Immediately after landing, the boxer pushes off with the right foot and jumps to the left-backward, performing the falling jump to the left-backward to return to a frontal stance facing his partner.

6. The boxer pushes off, jumping up and twisting counterclockwise 180 degrees so that he lands with his back to his partner.

7. Immediately after landing, the boxer makes a reverse jump clockwise, to return to a frontal stance facing his partner.

8. The boxer pushes off with the right foot and jumps to the left-forward with the left foot, performing the falling jump to the left-forward.

9. Immediately after landing, the boxer pushes off with the left foot and jumps to the right-backward, performing the falling jump to the right-backward to return to a frontal stance facing his partner.

10.   The boxer transfers his body weight to his right foot and performs the shuffle-twist to the right (counterclockwise), moving to the right flank.

11.   Immediately after landing, the boxer shifts his body weight to his left foot and performs the shuffle-twist to the left (clockwise), taking a frontal position.

12.   The boxer transfers his body weight to his left foot and performs the shuffle-twist to the left (clockwise), moving to the left flank.

13.   Immediately after landing, the boxer shifts his body weight to his right foot and performs the shuffle-twist to the right (counterclockwise), taking a frontal position.

Execution by Mike Tyson

Below is a snippet of Rooney and Tyson's jump practice. Tyson jumps, turning 180 degrees clockwise and landing with his back to Rooney. Next, Tyson immediately makes the second 180-degree counter-clockwise jump and lands facing Rooney. Immediately after landing, Tyson makes the falling jump to the right-forward, pushing off with his left foot and landing on the right foot.

Jumping rope

One of the basic exercises for developing boxing footwork is jumping rope. Learning how to jump rope is very important. This is regardless of whether you are boxing for fitness or fighting. It helps you improve your overall speed and gives your body a great workout. This exercise trains increased jumping ability and endurance. Through this exercise, the boxer's legs become like springs. This exercise determines increased jumping ability, agility, swiftness in attack, and speed of boxing. All this will put you in great shape as a boxer. Jumping rope will make your feet much faster. Tyson, despite his weight and physique, was good at this exercise.

Despite all the advantages of this exercise, only jumping rope does not allow a boxer to master the special techniques of peekaboo footwork. All boxers jump on the rope, but not every boxer knows the special techniques of footwork. Jumping rope only creates a good physical basis for mastering special footwork techniques.

Agility ladder for boxing

Recently in the boxing world, such a tool as an agility ladder for boxing has become popular. A boxer can improve boxing footwork and techniques with the agility ladder. The purpose of training on this tool is to develop jumping ability, endurance, and coordination. There are many jumps on the boxing ladder. An agility ladder allows training different boxing footwork drills. These drills could be used by beginners or advanced professionals in boxing.

In our opinion, it is reasonable to include in the training on the boxing ladder different techniques of peekaboo footwork to bring them to the automatism. Each boxer can independently develop the necessary exercises for training peekaboo footwork on the boxing agility ladder.

Made in the USA
Las Vegas, NV
21 February 2024

86058639R00144